A Troubled Affair

Essa Sims

Published by Essa Sims, 2025.

A TROUBLED AFFAIR

First edition. February 18, 2025.

ISBN: 979-8230567714

Written by Essa Sims.

Also by Essa Sims

Dark Adversary
Accident Prone
A Small World
A Troubled Affair

Chapter One

Shoulder-length golden hair swinging, Zoe hummed happily to herself and skipped nimbly aside as a lorry thundered through a kerbside puddle. Putting her hand out from under the umbrella, she realised that the downpour had finally eased. Folding the umbrella and shaking it, she noted as she neared her destination that the sun was finally breaking through the clouds. She turned into a quiet cul-de-sac, her footsteps slowing as she opened a small gate and walked up the neatly tiled path along to the entrance door of a small apartment block.

Zoe experienced a sense of trepidation as she climbed the stairs and approached the front door, but then she always experienced that when calling on her brother. Both she and her sister, Libby, never knew what state of chaos they would be greeted with on entering his flat. She had never met anybody who was so disorganised as Tom. His home would have made a good setting for the battle zone in a war film. He excused his untidiness as part of his artistic temperament, which sounded a bit flimsy to her because, strangely enough, this haphazard way of life fortunately didn't extend to his job. I suppose, she thought, smiling to herself, as long as he has two slaves to clear up for him, why would he bother?

Plain untidiness was bad enough, but every now and then her brother decided to pursue a new hobby. Unfortunately, this time it was do-it-yourself. He had decided to redecorate the flat and Tom being Tom, it would never occur to him to do one room at a time, so she was waiting to see what extra debris he had added to the untidy heap that it usually ended up in. Once a week Zoe turned up and with Libby's help, waded in and tried to restore some sort of order to his hovel. They sorted his clothes out, not all, just enough to keep him on the right side of decent. Tom, being the youngest, they had always felt it their duty to look after him and old habits die hard, even though he was a now grown man, but there was no way she and her sister were going to take on all his chores. He would be only too happy to let them do so, and they simply hadn't the time. Zoe had her own small apartment and job to cope with, as did Libby, and that kept both girls busy enough.

Their mother and father were comfortably off and when all three of their children had been ready to fly the nest, they had seen them off in style. Giving them a good start in their chosen fields, and each had done well for themselves. Then their parents had cunningly sold up, buying a much smaller house, making it impossible for their children to try and sneak back in.

"Escape, escape, I hear you cry," Zoe said jokingly, as they outlined their plans to their children.

"Now, darling, don't feel that you can't come home to stay," her mother, Cora, protested. adding mischievously. "Just not for too long. Seriously though Zoe, you know that you're welcome anytime, as are you two. Although I have to point out that it is a bit cramped in here."

She laughed as Zoe pulled a hurt face and picked her bag up, making forlornly for the door, with the other two not far behind her.

"The attic is cold, it's true, but quite usable," her father chimed in. He grinned. "I'm sure that we can fit that old narrow collapsible bed in there."

"I see through your false words," their daughter said, with a mock frown. "Don't be alarmed, but I might just take you up on the offer of the odd weekend in the attic and share a crust of dry bread with you."

"The bed is a bit narrow, but we could share," Libby giggled.

"I quite like dry bread," Tom offered, amiably.

In fact, the house, although small in comparison to their previous accommodation, was still spacious and had two large spare bedrooms.

Zoe knew that her parents would welcome any one of them to stay if they needed to, but she was also aware that they were glorying in their newfound sense of freedom, and it must be nice to only have themselves to think of for once.

"It's okay, mum," Zoe grinned. "I know you love us really, but us cuckoos know when we're beaten."

Her parents laughed with her. The Burgess clan had lived happily together, but the older couple had wondered for a while if their offspring would ever find partners and leave. As it happened, there were no partners as yet, but their children had flown eagerly when the opportunity had presented itself, now they all had their freedom to varying degrees.

When Zoe had been searching for a place to live, she could never seem to find a home within her price range that really appealed to her, and then she had seen it, the perfect cosy little nest. It was love at first sight. The apartment was in a quiet street, conveniently placed near a small row of local shops and was set in a small block set well back from the road. The building was only two stories high, and the apartment Zoe had chosen was on the top floor. An expanse of lawn and a horseshoe of green shrubs helped screen them from passing traffic. The bushes were beautifully maintained, and some were in full bloom, which just enhanced the appeal for her. As she had walked through the front door to view the place, the first thing that had confronted Zoe was the spiral staircase taking up a great deal of space in the box-like hall, but much to her delight and the deciding factor that clinched the sale was that it led up to a small attic room. It was tiny but adequate for her needs, and a roof light and side dormer window made the room bright and airy. Perfect for a studio.

Zoe worked in a design company specialising in hand-printed tiles, but what she really liked to do was to create jewellery, and painting the intricate designs that were required afforded her endless pleasure. Through contacts in the business, she had gradually built up a reputation for exquisite workmanship and now had enough commissions, and a nicely rounded bank account, to feel that she would soon be able to indulge in choosing exactly which path she wished to follow.

Her sister, Libby, who was two years younger, worked with animals and rented part of a small, terraced house near the veterinary surgery where she worked. At the moment she was a humble assistant but held ambitions to start her own animal sanctuary. It had been a dream of Libby's since she was a small child, and if Zoe knew her mother, she would be only too willing to help her daughter set one up when the time came.

Tom, her brother, was a sunny-natured man and the only time one would see him completely serious was when he was behind the camera. He was presently employed by a well-known film studio and was a top cameraman dedicated to his job and liked by all who worked with him. His career seemed to be set.

Zoe put her key in the lock and opened the door cautiously just in case something fell on her. Her brother had a habit of placing things right where one could either fall over them or into them, and she knew to her cost that it paid to tread warily. As it was, only a trained eye such as hers could detect if a human being had recently disturbed the trail of destruction and dust that confronted her. She sighed with frustration as she stood surrounded by his latest, 'good idea' and tried to find somewhere to put the shopping down. She squared her shoulders, feeling like a heroine fighting the never-ending battle against grime.

She picked her way gingerly through the empty cans and heaps of torn wallpaper, making space on the table by the simple expedient of sweeping everything onto the floor with her arm, then setting her burdens carefully down upon the cleared surface. There was a layer of dust covering every surface from where he had scraped the walls to remove the wallpaper, and she grimaced as she looked down at her jacket. She had a great deal of it on her sleeve from off the table.

Tom's old denim jacket, draped carelessly on the floor, gave away the fact that her brother was at home. He never went anywhere without it. His security blanket, their mother called it.

"Tom," she called, repeating his name a little louder when there was no reply. Then Zoe spotted the bathroom door standing ajar and heard the shower running. She frowned and wondered if he was all right. It wasn't like him to leave the door open. She approached the door hesitantly and pushing it wider and keeping her eyes averted from the cubicle, leaned inside. "Tom," she called again, and then her eyes were caught by the electric blue and yellow uniform draped over the bath stool.

She picked it up, her face puzzled, saw the motif on the front and her eyes widened. She smiled, another souvenir from the set. How had he managed to snaffle this treasure? Libby would be absolutely thrilled because it was from her latest crush.

Zoe tapped lightly on the frosted shower screen. It slid open slowly and to her horror, instead of her brother's familiar face, a handsome muscular stranger put his head out and her smile rapidly shrivelled. Her eyes rounded as they made a rapid journey of the powerful torso that was also emerging.

"Oh, I'm sorry," she mumbled, averting her eyes as she made a hasty exit, slamming the door shut behind her. She put her hand to her head in disbelief. What was she apologising for? He was the one who had some explaining to do! She frowned, there was something about his face that tugged at her memory. Then it dawned on her, as recognition kicked in.

"Good, I see you've cleared the table." Her brother appeared from the kitchen, a tray in his hands. He looked up and registered her flustered state. "What's up with you?"

"Tom! Do you know who that is in the shower?" Zoe was leaning back against the bathroom door gasping, both hands pressed to her hot cheeks.

"Yeah, some guy I met on the set. He needed to get away for some reason, so I offered him coffee and a shower. Seems quite nice."

"No, I mean do you realise who he is?" she hissed.

Tom shook his head. "Jack something or other," he said vaguely as he bent to place the tray of food and coffee onto the table.

"For goodness sake," she spluttered, "don't you recognise 'Tronicman' when you see him?"

"Tronicman?" he repeated, raising his brows with a mystified look.

"You know, big muscular guy, blue and yellow suit, wreaks vengeance on the baddies," she said, emphasising each word, "very similar to the big muscular hunk of man in your shower."

Now she had his full attention as dawning comprehension entered his eyes. They were interrupted by the insistent ring of the doorbell. It would be their sister, Libby, come to do her share of clearing up the bomb damage and she was late, as usual.

Zoe was nearly knocked down as she opened the door and her sister rushed by her. "Guess who's in town?" Libby said with a breathless giggle, pressing her hand dramatically to her heart.

"Now let me see, ah, yes." Zoe had a fair inkling to whom her sister was referring and smirked, as she pointed her finger at the closed door behind her. "Your favourite hunk is stark naked behind that door."

"I wish." Libby laughed uproariously. Her laughter died away in a strangled gurgle as the door opened and a tall, bronzed man emerged, wearing nothing but a towel draped loosely around his waist, looking absolutely stunning. Jack Hammell in all his glory, well almost.

Libby managed to start breathing again, while Tom stared at him, feeling as though his own skin had been bleached, as he observed the expanse of rippling golden flesh, feeling suitably envious of the broad chest and bulging muscles that confronted him.

"Coffee here, when you want it," he said faintly.

"Hi!" Jack grinned, baring a set of dazzling white teeth on seeing their dumbstruck faces.

"I'm sorry, man," Tom said, really looking at him this time, "I didn't recognise you; it's the suit and eye mask. I only know you when you're wearing them."

"See, it really works," Jack laughed, "I become invisible without it, which is just the way I like it."

Zoe had recovered from her initial embarrassment, but not the awesome spectacle of a Hollywood star in her brother's small living room. She had known that the latest 'Tronicman' adventure film was being made, Tom had told them so, but it hadn't interested her very much at the time, and now they actually had the 'warrior for good' lunching with them. How about that! She pulled herself together and poured the star some coffee, trying not to stare at him, and lowering her lashes to mask her fascinated interest. So, this was Jack Hammell, the man women lusted after.

He had first starred in a popular US soap that Libby had watched avidly, and she had been inconsolable when the series had been axed, and over the moon when he had been chosen to play the part of "Tronicman'. The films had been an enormous success, partly because of the hype; it was surely not because of the acting, but mostly because of Jack's on-screen charisma. He was devastatingly good-looking, women chased after him in droves, and men strove to be just like him. Zoe had to admit that in the flesh he was pretty awesome, and he was certainly a gorgeous specimen, yet for some reason, he didn't push any buttons for her. Not that Zoe didn't find him attractive; he seemed to fill the room, exuding a potent masculine aura that made her stare at him with feminine appreciation. She would have to be dead not to feel the pull of his presence, and her poor sister was positively drooling.

"Sit, make yourself comfortable," Zoe said to Jack, trying to act nonchalantly and leaning closer, whispered. "Although you would probably feel better if you put some clothes on. At least my sister would."

He glanced across at Libby, who was still standing mesmerised, her brown eyes large in her small heart shaped face as she gazed at him, and Jack gave a lazy smile. "Okay, maybe you're right." He turned to her brother. "Perhaps you have something that might fit me, Tom?"

"Oh, right, follow me Mr T." He looked the hulking young star up and down. "Hmm, my gear might be a bit tight on you, the only thing I've got that could possibly fit are baggy running trousers and a loose T-shirt."

"Lead me to them," Jack smiled.

When they'd disappeared into the bedroom and shut the door firmly behind them, Zoe hissed at her sister. "For pity's sake, Lib, pull yourself together. He probably thinks that you aren't capable of speech. You look like a fish with your mouth open like that."

Her sister snapped out of her trance and laughed delightedly. "Oh, my God! Wow, wow, wow! How did he turn up here of all places? I can't believe this, my hero in the flesh, and what fabulous flesh." She clasped her hands to her chest and breathed ecstatically. "This can't be happening. I know that I put an order in for him, but I didn't believe for one moment that it would really come true and to deliver him here to me personally, perfect."

"Control yourself," Zoe laughed, "If wishes came true that easily, we would be falling over the piled-up bodies of all the gorgeous men that you've ever fancied."

She was still smiling as her brother and Jack reappeared. The star was now modestly covered in Tom's clothing, though it amused her to observe the way he managed to make even those garments look sexy as they pulled across his broad chest and thighs. Even Tom was eyeing them with a frown, wondering why the garments had never looked quite the same on him. When they were seated with their coffee and rolls, Libby managed to tear her eyes away from the actor long enough to question Tom.

"Surely you must have guessed that Jack here was in the film you were working on, even in a minor role?"

"Actually," her brother grinned, "I really didn't think about who was playing the lead."

"How about the suit Jack was wearing," Zoe broke in, "Didn't that tell you anything?"

"It was the long overcoat Jack wore," he shrugged. "It covered him so well, and anyway I was making coffee when he removed his outer garments and went to take a shower."

"Yes, but *bright yellow boots*," Libby rolled her eyes. "That didn't strike you as odd?"

"You get some eccentric types on set," Tom excused himself. He looked apologetically at Jack. "Sorry once again, but I don't take a lot of notice of actors when I'm behind the camera. They're just players in my viewfinder.

"That's what I liked about you," Jack smiled, "you really had no idea of who I was, yet you offered me hospitality. Most people usually have an ulterior motive for getting close to me. I knew as soon as I spoke to you that you didn't know me from Adam."

"I'm never going to live this down back at work." Tom threw his head back and laughed. "They think I'm oblivious enough as it is."

"Is he always like this?" Jack turned to Zoe with an amused smile.

"Oh, yes, he's always bringing home waifs and strays, they seem to gravitate towards him." She flushed as she realised how that might sound. "Sorry, I didn't mean to imply that you were a stray exactly..." Her voice trailed off as she became aware that she was starting to babble, his presence still causing a certain amount of awed shyness on her part.

"Don't worry about it," Jack laughed, "I know just what you mean, and I'm grateful that Tom was kind enough to give me the chance to escape with him. Sometimes it's so good to get away and just be me. Not that I'm knocking the part. The role has brought me recognition and a good living, but sometimes I need a breather, a bolthole."

He looked around at their friendly faces with a sense of pleasure; he could get to like these folks very much. There was no adulation in their expressions, a slightly overawed air maybe, he could understand that and a not unnatural curiosity. Even Libby, now that she'd gotten over her initial shock, was just regarding him with a woman's keen interest for a well-made man. Jack found himself caught by that look and felt a stirring of interest. Libby was a pretty girl, with long curly brown hair framing her face, expressive eyes, and an appealing mouth. She was also a confident girl, always smiling, which usually made people want to smile back, and he found himself wanting that smile to be directed solely at him. Hey, where did that come from?

Zoe noted the look passing between them and felt a frisson of alarm, knowing that nothing could possibly come of any attraction that Libby might feel. She could only get hurt by such a relationship and Jack would drift off to pastures new. It was the nature of his job and the type of man he was.

Jack, glancing at her, felt irritated by the snap judgement on her easy-to-read face. Who was she to say what his innermost feelings were in regard to women, or how serious his intentions were? He was tired of the endless succession of starlets who vied for his attention just to climb a little higher on the ladder of fame. He didn't regard himself as promiscuous, but even he had to admit that his list of girlfriends was a fairly prodigious one. Now as he gazed at Libby, he felt something within himself responding that he had never experienced before, and given the chance, he would like to explore this new sensation.

Jack looked back at Zoe and for some reason, his cousin Daniel popped into his head. A mischievous smile curved his lips. What if he arranged for them to get together? He had every intention of seeing Libby again, with or without her sister's approval, so he would have plenty of time to arrange a meeting between the two. He studied Zoe. She was an attractive girl and seemed equally as strong-minded as his cousin, yet very feminine. She was serious and also appeared to have a good sense of humour. His cousin, on the other hand, was a large bear of a man, arrogant and overwhelming. He had never succumbed to such a weak emotion like love and scoffed at those who did. Daniel conducted his infrequent affairs like business deals, so naturally, they never lasted, and as for humour, he didn't appear to have any. Jack had a feeling that in this woman, his cousin would meet his match, and he chuckled fiendishly to himself.

The conversation flowed freely, and they found Jack scintillating company, Zoe watched him as he laughed and talked, completely relaxed. It amazed her that this humorous likeable man seated at their table was so unspoilt by success. She asked him whereabouts in America he lived. She was curious to know more about this intriguing man.

"My country is Canada. I was born and brought up there, and it's the place I call home. America is just a base while I'm filming, although it's a great place to spend time in, and I've made some lifelong friends there." His parents lived in Northern Canada, and he still made plenty of trips up to see them when he could, he informed them. "Daniel has a place near them, but he's mostly based in London because of his business."

"Daniel?" Zoe queried. "Your brother?"

"My cousin. He's a couple of years older than me, but we're very close. More like brothers, I suppose," he told her. He pushed his chair back and stood up reluctantly, not wanting to leave the relaxing company. He sighed, freedom never lasted long, and he had to get back on set, as did Tom. "Well, folks, thanks again for the visit, reminded me of home for a minute there." He threw his costume over his arm with a theatrical flourish and patted it, seeing Tom's grin. "I know, guys, sad isn't it how grown men make money, but believe me," he grimaced, "it helps pay the rent."

When the men had departed, Libby flung herself dejectedly down onto a wallpaper-covered chair. “He's gone, just like that,” she moaned. “No promises to see us again.”

Zoe laughed at her disgruntled face; she had to admit that the atmosphere had fallen flat after the virile young man had departed. People like that rarely entered one's life, let alone stayed in it. The whole episode seemed surreal, and they had only offered coffee and rolls to a top star! The food must have seemed meagre fare to what Jack was used to eating for lunch. Not that there had been a choice, because it was all they had.

“Why would he want to see us again? Apart from anything else, I should imagine that he has quite a busy schedule.” She looked down at Libby's forlorn figure. “This is one of those once-in-a-lifetime happenings. Just think, you can live on the, ‘I met a star in the flesh,’ story for years, and you saw plenty of it.”

“Mm, I sure did, and he is totally gorgeous. I have the strangest feeling that we're destined to meet again,” her sister said with conviction and folded her arms frowning up at her.

Zoe gazed at her with concern, Libby's crush must be more intense than she'd thought, and she didn't want her sister to harbour false hopes. “You might as well forget about it,” she cautioned. “Keep it for your dreams. Anyway, what happened to Peter?”

“Oh, him! I only went out with him twice, and he started planning our wedding. I mean, for heaven's sake, we hardly knew each other. That was a hard one to end. He was so upset, and I hated hurting him, but he was so persistent. Why can't things work out the way we wish them to?” Libby looked guilty and sighed soulfully. Her regretful mood didn't last, and she started to giggle. “All I'm asking for is that one of Hollywood's top hunks drops all those incredibly drop-dead gorgeous girls and chooses little old me.”

They both laughed out loud at this impossible dream. The laughter died when Tom came home later and told them about the invitation.

"Really?! Like in a showbiz party," Libby squealed, "all that glamour. Oh, God! What shall I wear and what about my hair?" She dropped the large bag of rubbish that she'd collected, and her eyes became glazed as Libby mentally ran through her wardrobe. "Nope, it's no good, I haven't a thing to wear. I'll have to go on a shopping spree."

Zoe sat down slowly, letting the dustpan and brush slide to the floor. It had taken Libby and her all their time just to make the place look habitable, heaven knows what Jack must have thought of it. On the other hand, he can't have been too appalled or he wouldn't have extended this invitation to them, and she felt suitably gratified that he had liked them well enough to do so. She really didn't want to go to the party, it wasn't her thing, although she had to confess to a certain degree of curiosity as to what the gathering would be like. She thought of her small selection of dresses and felt relieved. Problem solved; she had nothing remotely glamorous enough to wear.

Tom, who had been watching her, saw the determined look forming on her face and decided to head her off, he knew just how to manipulate Zoe. "Jack would be offended if any one of us didn't turn up," he said, with a plaintive air, "He specifically asked that we be there, and I promised him we would all accept." There, that would get her. His sister wouldn't dream of letting anybody down.

"That was an obvious ploy, Tom, but it worked." Zoe clicked her tongue and gave him an exasperated look. "I would never have put my order in for a baby brother if I'd known he would turn out to be you."

"Low blows work," Tom grinned unrepentantly. "Seriously though, sis, he really is looking forward to meeting you two again."

"I'll bet," she grumbled, wondering if Jack would even notice that she was there when he set eyes on Libby again.

ᘎᘎᘎᘎᘎᘎᘎ

Her sister persuaded Zoe to buy a new dress for the occasion and made a point of going with her, just to make sure that she chose something a little more daring than her usual style. When Zoe tried the dress on that Libby had picked out for her, she was aghast at the amount of breast it exposed and was inclined to tear it off again.

"Don't you dare," Libby warned, "you look positively beautiful in it."

"I want people to look at my face when I'm talking, not my chest," Zoe protested, as she fussed with the delicately thin straps, making sure that they were straight, and more to the point, able to hold her in place. They did look a bit flimsy.

"Wait until you see mine," her sister laughed, then stopped as she saw the frown forming on Zoe's face. "Only kidding. Anyway, I should imagine you'll probably look quite modestly dressed compared to some of the other women there, believe me."

Libby bullied her into buying the dress, keeping a close eye on the transaction, in case her sister sneakily slid it back onto the hangar and changed it. Then Libby dragged her around yet more shops, as she had now decided that Zoe simply must buy new shoes and a small evening bag to match the dress, which lightened her sister's purse considerably.

When she arrived back home, Zoe tried the dress on again in the privacy of her bedroom and realised that her sister was right, it had been worth splashing out for. She preened in front of the mirror, it really did look good and perhaps, given time, she would get used to that amount of cleavage showing. Zoe stared at her reflection; she would never be beautiful. Lovely would have done. Attractive was what she settled for and felt secretly pleased at her image. Her eyes were large and light blue, set in a rounded face, and her nose was pert. A man's gaze tended to linger on her lips, which were full and enticing. She didn't possess the same curly hair as Libby, which she rather envied. Hers was straight and blonde and cut to shoulder length. Nothing to draw a man's attention, or so she thought.

Chapter Two

On the evening of the party, they gathered once again at Tom's flat, and both sisters were dumbstruck as they stood regarding their suddenly handsome brother clad in a beautifully cut dinner jacket, with crisp white shirt and bow tie.

"My God, who is this handsome stranger?" Zoe laughed. "Can this be my hideously untidy brother I see before me?" She looked him up and down, seeing for the first time what his numerous girlfriends had been drawn to. Tom had a sensitive face, lean and attractive, his light brown hair matched his sparkling eyes, and his mouth seemed to sport a permanent half-smile. Yes, her brother was quite a catch, as long as the woman who caught him could keep up with the pit that he lived in.

"You are my favourite brother." She smiled at him fondly.

"The answer to that is obvious," he chuckled, "so I won't say it."

They both grinned and Libby laughed as she grabbed their arms and pushed them towards the door. "Come on, we're supposed to be there in half an hour, and if we don't get a move on, we're going to be late."

ꟷꟷꟷ

The first thing that hit them when the two burly guards opened the doors and let them through was the deafening noise. The club that Jack had commandeered for the event was quite exclusive, yet as Zoe was to discover, it was not only the rougher elements that could be badly behaved. Drink was flowing freely; some people were becoming over-boisterous, and tempers were beginning to fray.

"God! I've only been here a quarter of an hour and things are getting out of hand already," she muttered. She turned away from the fight that had now erupted in front of her and looked frantically around for her brother and sister who had become separated from her by the press of people. She hated unpleasantness and felt a twinge of fear as one of the men bumped into her. The antagonist's actions only consisted of pushing and shoving at the moment, but by the belligerent expressions on both faces, it could well escalate. Her searching eyes were caught by the exceptionally large, dark-haired man leaning against the wall, hands in pockets, surveying the scene with a faintly sardonic smile. If he was a bouncer, he wasn't doing a very good job of it, she thought angrily. Why was he lounging about when he ought to be attending to his duty? Someone could get hurt.

Zoe fought her way around the edge of the crowd, marched up and planted herself in front of him. "Can't you see what's happening right there in front of you?" she hissed up at him. "You're paid good money for this job, now go and sort that lot out, or I'll report you for dereliction of duty."

He stared down in amazement at the small figure standing in front of him. She had actually poked him in the chest between each word. His gaze roved over her and Zoe was made very aware of the inadequate neckline on her dress. She found herself pulling at it, trying to cover her swelling breasts.

"Well?" she prompted him, strangely breathless.

"Right," he said slowly, withdrawing his hands from his pockets. He straightened up, and moving her gently aside, he bulldozed his way through the milling bodies. The man confronted the troublemakers, who to her amazement, seemed to melt away as if by magic, within minutes.

Zoe, watching him as he dealt swiftly with the problem, found herself fascinated by his sheer size. Her skin still tingled where his heavy hands had rested and she found herself pressing her own hands against her chest, as the man strode back towards her. Now she wondered how she'd had the temerity to order him about. This guy looked as though he could crush her with one finger.

My God, he is so big, Zoe thought, as he towered over her. The breadth of his shoulders stretched the material of the expensive suit, but it was his face that arrested her attention. He was a ruggedly handsome man, deeply tanned, with the most beautiful eyes she had ever seen on any male. They were a clear sparkling green framed by thick black lashes, and his heavy slumberous lids gave them an incredibly sexual appeal. His nose was strong and slightly hooked, as befitted such a face. As for his mouth, she felt a shiver run down her spine as her eyes lingered on it. His lips curled slightly at the edges as though he were about to smile, and his firm top lip was balanced by the full lower one. Zoe felt her heart beat a little faster as his mouth parted, revealing near-perfect white teeth.

"Good enough for you?" he inquired silkily.

"Pardon?" she flushed, wondering if he could read minds.

"Have I earned my money?" He inclined his head towards the now peaceful scene before her.

She nodded her head, not trusting her voice, and began rummaging through her small evening bag. Luckily, Zoe always made a point of keeping some spare cash on her, and not just her card. It came in handy at times, like now for instance. She looked up and cleared her throat on encountering his green eyes watching her with an intensity that was positively unnerving.

"Here, please take this, and thank you." She hurriedly made her departure, disappearing into the crowded room and he was left staring at the crumpled money in his hand with a bemused expression on his face.

By the end of the evening, she was relieved to get home, and as soon as she got through the door, she made a beeline for the kitchen, making coffee for them all before they went their separate ways. She carried the tray back into the living room, setting it down carefully onto her small table and picked her own cup up gratefully.

"If that's a showbiz party, I'm glad that we're not invited to many of them," Zoe sighed, as she slumped into her favourite armchair.

"Oh, don't be such a party pooper," Libby giggled, still glowing with excitement. She looked down at her sister's inert body with a shake of the head. "You're no fun. I still feel like dancing. Wasn't it wonderful?"

"It was certainly different," Zoe agreed, trying to stifle a tired yawn.

"Did you see how many stars were there?" her sister enthused, her eyes sparkling with awe, and didn't Jack look fabulously handsome?"

"Yes, he did look good, I must admit." Zoe laughed up at Libby's shining face, "and it was quite enjoyable up to a point, but what about those morons who were causing all that trouble?"

"What trouble?"

Her sister's puzzled face made Zoe roll her eyes. How could she have not noticed that noisy altercation taking place? "Don't tell me that you never saw or heard all that commotion coming from that group of people in the middle of the floor?"

"Nope. What happened?" Libby said, her face more serious now. She shrugged at the look of disbelief on her sister's face. "I'm sorry, but Jack and I were out on the balcony, and what with everybody talking and laughing at the top of their voices, we couldn't hear much of what was going on inside, I'm afraid."

It was what else had been occupying them that worried Zoe. She just hoped that her sister was not taking this flirtation too seriously. "It doesn't matter anyway," she sighed, "the bouncer went and sorted it out."

Her mind conjured him up and Zoe felt hot as she remembered his touch, his large warm hands. She had spent most of the evening furtively sneaking looks around, trying to locate him again, but with no luck. She shook herself impatiently, anyone would think that she'd never seen a good-looking man before. On the other hand, there was handsome, and then there was drop-dead gorgeous, oozing sex appeal. Grow up, she told herself impatiently. There was probably very little beneath that presentable surface. She felt heat run sharply through her. Now she was imagining him naked. Where were all these rampant thoughts coming from? Maybe she was simply tired, or feeling the march of time, and she was searching for a man to end her spinsterhood. The call of nature to make a nest. Or was that only for the birds? Heavens, there was plenty of time before taking on a man and all that entailed. Loss of freedom, having to tend to someone else's needs, sharing! Not yet, thank you.

She jumped up and marched into the kitchen, slamming cupboards and rattling cups as she washed up. Tom put his head around the door. "If that's a hint, don't worry, we're going."

"Sorry, I was deep in thought." Zoe laughed at his mock fear. "I would have thrown you out soon anyway. I need my sleep."

Later, as she stood cleaning her teeth, Zoe paused, thinking of the way the man had stared down at her with those mesmerising eyes. Now that she came to think of it, his expression had been a strange mixture of shock and humour. Why? Then she also recalled the way that she'd poked his chest in her anxiety, and she flushed with embarrassment. He probably thought that she was one of those spoilt drama queens that she had met so many of this evening. Zoe shrugged, oh, well, at least she'd given him a good tip, although why he had stared at the money as though he had never seen any before, baffled her.

Over the next few days, Zoe was able to push the party and that man to the back of her mind. Her work kept her busy and a new commission put enough pressure on to keep her occupied until late into each evening.

Libby had been staying with Zoe for the last few days, the excuse being that she had taken a leaf out of their brother's book and was redecorating her rented rooms, but Zoe wasn't deceived. The truth was that her sister was nearer to Tom's place with the chance to bump into Jack. Tom was bemused by his sudden popularity and wondered what he had done to deserve such constant attention from his sister.

When Libby was not around at his flat, she moped about the place, lounging back on the sofa or staring out of the window, constantly jumping up and making coffee. It was obvious that her carefully laid plans were not working, because so far Libby hadn't seen Jack once, and it seemed as though she never would. Her endless chatter about the man began to get on Zoe's nerves, but she was literally saved by the bell when Tom rang and informed them that Jack would be calling in on him that evening, and perhaps Libby would like to come over for a visit, Jack having apparently dropped a large hint to that effect.

Zoe watched as her sister reached near panic level while she debated as to what to wear, and heaved a sigh of relief later that evening when the younger girl finally closed the door behind her. Solitude had become a rare occurrence with her sister about and Zoe threw herself happily down into a chair with a bowl of her favourite ice cream. There were some occasions when one had to give in to temptation, and this was one of them.

ᘓᘓᘓᘓᘓᘓᘓ

During the next few weeks, Jack became a constant visitor to Tom's flat, as did Libby, and their romance progressed at a steady rate. It had now developed from a light-hearted flirtation into a steadier relationship, and Zoe watched these proceedings with growing apprehension.

Libby had persuaded Tom to invite Jack over for dinner and was now beside herself with a mixture of excitement and anxiety, in case it all went disastrously wrong. Zoe could hear the loud clatter of pans as her sister, who was downstairs, prepared a meal. Libby had insisted that she could manage by herself, and Zoe had taken her at her word, although why they seemed to have ended up at her flat was a mystery to her. She could have sworn she had said no when Libby asked. She was driving Zoe mad, causing her to spend far more time shut away in her studio just to gain a little peace, but this evening there was no shutting out the noise from below.

As usual, despite the distraction, Zoe became deeply absorbed in her work and lost track of time, with the result that she felt particularly weary as she stumbled down from the attic. She wanted nothing more than a nice soothing shower and a strong cup of coffee. She became aware of deep laughter as she descended the stairs and groaned with annoyance. She had completely forgotten about the meal and could really do without the hassle of company right now. She was hesitating on the bottom step, contemplating a swift return to her studio, when the decision was taken out of her hands as her sister opened the hall door and spotted her skulking there.

"There you are, I was just going to give you a call. There's a drink ready and you must come and meet Jack's cousin. Come on," Libby frowned as her sister still hovered on the step. "It would be rude not to acknowledge him, especially as I said I was coming to fetch you."

"All right," Zoe gave in gracefully. She glanced down at her paint-smeared baggy top, and tight black leggings. Her hair was an untidy mess where she had constantly pushed her fingers through it. She also knew that her face was shiny and smudged with paint. "But I'm hardly dressed for visitors, am I?"

"Honestly, Zoe, you can be such a pain at times. You knew they were coming. Why didn't you go and get changed earlier?" Libby admonished her.

"Sorry, I forgot all about it. Oh! who cares," Zoe said, grumpily, as she followed her sister back into the room. 'I do, I do,' she moaned to herself as she came to an abrupt halt.

Facing her and dominating the room stood the tall dark man from the party and it was patently obvious to her now that he was no bouncer. Libby ushered her over to him. "Daniel, this is my sister, Zoe," she said, pulling her reluctant sister forward. "Zoe, this is Daniel, Jack's cousin."

Having introduced them, Libby felt her duty over and left them to get acquainted. "Hi," he drawled, his lips pulling up into a mocking smile, as he stepped forward and engulfed her small hand in his, squeezing it firmly. The warmth from his hand seemed to be travelling up her arm and she shivered. She could now see the resemblance between the two cousins. It was so strong that she couldn't believe she'd missed it before, and the Canadian accent should have given her some clue to the relationship. Did he recognise her? It was possible, in her dishevelled state, that he didn't, and she hoped that was the case. He had made no reference to the party as yet, but he was giving her a strangely penetrating look, and he showed no signs of relinquishing her hand. His grip, if anything, was tightening.

Daniel stared down at her, shocked at the sudden primal urge to scoop her up and spirit her away to some dark hiding place. He let go of her hand as though it had burnt him. What the hell was wrong with him? She was just another woman, damn it, and an extremely scruffy one at that. He had never entertained such primitive thoughts before. Sexual, yes, but this strange jealousy that reared up at the thought that she could be the attraction for his cousin was alien to him. He hardly knew the woman, yet he had not forgotten her. Why the hell not?

He turned sharply away, meeting Jack's speculative eyes and frowned at him, but his cousin merely smiled, including him in the conversation with Tom. It would have seemed churlish to walk away. As Daniel stood listening to the two men talk, he feigned an interest, trying to push Zoe out of his mind, but he was acutely aware of her across the room. It was as though his inner being was attuned to her presence, and he felt threatened by that unsettling fact.

Zoe felt totally embarrassed by his abrupt snub. He had turned away as though she was unwholesome, and she felt outraged by his rudeness. She knew that she wasn't at her best, being dishevelled and paint spattered, and that in the world he moved in, he was probably used to much more glamorous women, but there was no need to act as though she wasn't even worth being polite to.

Libby set the food down on the table and beckoned Zoe over. "Isn't he scrumptious, what do you think?"

"Who?" Zoe helped her with the plates and pretended an interest in the settings.

"You know perfectly well who I mean," Libby giggled. "He's too big to miss."

"He's okay, I suppose, a bit too overwhelmingly masculine for my taste though, and his manners could do with some attention. I find him quite disagreeable," Zoe sniffed.

"Disagreeable, Daniel?" Libby stared at her as if she had uttered some blasphemy. The puzzled look in her eyes changed to understanding as she noted the slight flush on her sister's face. They were interrupted as the men came to take their places. Jack was amused to note that his cousin and Zoe hardly exchanged a word unless forced to do so and avoided eye contact whenever possible. This was so unlike Daniel; he was a man who could always handle any given situation, and women usually presented no problem to him at all. It was all going far better than he could have hoped. He stared at his cousin, getting a sinful glee out of the other man's discomfort.

As soon as he decently could, Daniel proffered his excuses and made a hasty departure, promising to call again sometime. "Not if I can help it," he muttered to himself as he stampeded down the stairs, "I can do without these sorts of complications in my life." He sighed with relief as he gained the sanctity of his car, glad that as soon as this damn film was over, his cousin would be flying back to America, and his own life could return to normal. There would be no more of these ghastly people to meet.

He felt a flash of guilt. That was too sweeping a judgement, and to be fair, most of the actors he had met were very nice people, as these people appeared to be. It was just the few who sought to draw attention to themselves that drove him mad. For instance, that menace of a woman, Janine Somers, a would-be top Hollywood star. She had already risen quite high in the glitzy world of show business and had decided, for some unfathomable reason, that she wanted him, when she had the choice of so many good-looking men who inhabited the same world as herself.

Daniel didn't realise quite what a handsome man he was. With his height and breadth, he could have easily fitted in with her lifestyle and probably would have been snapped up eagerly by some talent scout if he'd had the slightest interest in the acting world, which he didn't. He found the whole scenario irksome; his business came first, and Janine came nowhere.

She was a lovely girl to look at, yet she held no interest or even sex appeal for Daniel. Her nature, it seemed to him, was shallow and she courted publicity with a single-minded determination that filled him with distaste. One thing he did expect in the women he occasionally escorted was a decent conversation, and Janine simply wasn't capable of it. Of course, the more unattainable he was, the more he appealed to the predatory side of her nature, and she wouldn't be shaken off. With the result that everywhere he went, she contrived to be. The inevitable result was compromising photographs appearing in the local and national newspapers. Janine usually managed to plaster herself all over him just as a photographer happened, by a strange coincidence, to be passing by. Now he was really getting fed up with the whole situation, and Daniel snorted with disgust as he put his key in the ignition. Nothing happened. He tried again several times, with the same result. He snatched his phone from his pocket impatiently and tried to make a call. Even that wouldn't work, and he began to wonder if fate was conspiring against him.

"Oh, God!" He slumped forward and rested his head on the steering wheel. "Please don't make me have to go back in there."

A strange fear invaded him as he slowly climbed the stairs to the apartment and rang the bell. He had a horrible premonition of impending doom. The door swung open, and Tom stood regarding him with a puzzled frown.

"What's up?"

"My car, damn thing won't start, and my phone has just died on me. Do you think I could ring for a taxi?"

"Sure, come on in." Tom held the door open and ushered him inside. "You might as well have another coffee while you wait."

To Daniel's relief, there was no sign of Zoe, and he allowed himself to relax as he made his call. He put the phone back down, and as he turned, he sucked his breath in, feeling as though he had received a blow to the stomach. From where he was standing, Daniel directly faced a bedroom door, and it was slightly ajar. There was his torment, laying sprawled on the bed in a sound sleep, her blonde hair spread out in tangled disarray over her pillow, and the sheet had slipped down, exposing her scantily clad body to his hot gaze. Her night dress was hardly adequate to be called such, and where it had ridden up, it exposed long slender legs. The flimsy straps had slipped off her shoulders and Daniel felt a flush suffuse his face as he gazed at her soft breasts, barely covered by a thin network of lace. His heart began to thud heavily as his eyes were drawn to the parted moistness of her mouth, and suddenly he wanted nothing more in the world than to feel those lips parting beneath his. He turned away abruptly, rubbing his hand over his face and cursing under his breath, ashamed of his furtive ogling. Just instant lust, he thought.

Tom brought him his coffee, which he drank in one gulp, burning his mouth as a result. He refused a seat and waited impatiently by the door for his taxi, hardly speaking.

"What the hell is wrong with you?" His cousin's irate voice made him jump, as it penetrated his black mood. Daniel turned around and found himself staring into Jack's frowning face. "These people are my friends," Jack hissed. "Your boorish attitude is bordering on insulting. You may not approve of them, but they have been extremely good to me. Don't treat them as though they're not worth cultivating."

Daniel stared at him, feeling an acute sense of embarrassment at his own uncharacteristic behaviour. "Make my apologies," he said quietly. "No insult intended, I assure you, Jack. Just some business deal bothering me, that's all, no reflection on them."

He was more effusive in his goodbyes than he would normally have been, and guilt made him want to atone for his odd manner. As a result, he found himself invited, much against his will, to dinner the next weekend. The refusal that sprang to his lips was quickly swallowed as he caught his cousin's watchful eye. Consequently, when Daniel walked down to get into the taxi, he felt as though he had been press-ganged.

When Zoe heard of the forthcoming dinner, she was horrified and frantically tried to find a reason not to be there. "Oh, Libby, I can't face him."

"Why, what's so terrible about Daniel?" Her sister frowned at her. "True, he is a bit aloof, but he really does seem a nice enough guy. It's only a dinner and you don't even have to speak to him if you don't want to. Anyway, Jack asked Dan's girlfriend to come, as well, so don't worry. He probably won't even notice you."

"In that case, I might as well not be there," Zoe put in quickly, but by the look on her sister's face, she wasn't going to get off that easily. For some reason, the mention of a girlfriend filled Zoe with irrational jealousy. Heck, she didn't even like the man and five minutes ago she was trying to get out of going. He could go out with whom he pleased, she sniffed, and yet that niggling feeling of discontent wouldn't go away.

Zoe couldn't understand herself, she'd had boyfriends before, one or two, nothing serious. She never let it go too far, something had always held her back, a sense of things not right in the relationship, and now she was going weak at the knees for someone completely unsuitable. In fact, he didn't even like her. Yet being near him made the sexual predator inside Zoe roar to get out. How pathetic can I get, she groaned, especially in view of who his girlfriend had turned out to be; the extremely glamorous star, Janine Somers. She was loath to admit that she was so attracted to such an aloof man, and the less she saw of him the better.

ꞁꞁꞁꞁꞁꞁꞁ

The day of the dinner came around all too soon and a mound of clothes gradually piled up on Zoe's bed as she tried on everything that she possessed yet still found nothing suitable to wear. Giving up, she grabbed her purse and set off for the nearest town to purchase a new dress, although why she was going to so much trouble, she couldn't fathom. It took her all afternoon and the saleswoman in the last shop was as pleased as she was when Zoe finally settled on the dress that she'd tried on in the first place. By this time, she was hot, fed up, and couldn't wait to get home and have a nice refreshing shower.

That evening, as she surveyed herself in the mirror, she was reasonably satisfied by her reflection. The dress was a simple dark red sheath with double spaghetti thin straps, the delicately lacy hem came to just above her knees and it hugged her figure without clinging too tightly. She had brushed her hair vigorously until it crackled and flowed, silky soft, in a golden stream resting on her shoulders. She touched her face with a little more make up than usual and kept her jewellery simple, just a thin diamante necklace, matching bracelet, and small ear drops.

Zoe knew she looked as good as she could get, but there was no way she could even begin to compete with someone like Janine Somers. People like that only had to enter a room to monopolise it and all the men around. Janine could handle them so effortlessly and Zoe couldn't help the twinge of envy that she experienced. She was completely unaware of just how pretty she looked in the silky well-cut dress. She may not be as overtly glamorous as Janine, but she looked equally as appealing in a more delicate way.

Zoe stared at herself, feeling deflated and wondering why she had even bothered to dress up, especially when Libby had first informed her just who his girlfriend was, and now she was attending this party. You're doing it for yourself, she said sternly to her image, then she straightened her shoulders and walked into the living room, glancing around at the table, and nodding with satisfaction. She told herself that she was calm yet couldn't help the startled jump she gave when the sudden ring of the doorbell sounded. She rushed out into the small kitchen and busied herself, leaving Libby to open the door. The thought of having two top stars in her modest flat was almost too much to take in.

"Hi, beautiful," Jack's deep voice chimed.

Zoe shivered as she heard another deeper voice join in the greeting, followed by the unmistakable simpering tones of Janine. She heard her sister giggle as Jack whispered something to her, and Zoe smiled. He really was a very nice man despite his star status and seemed to be genuinely fond of Libby. Her worries on that score had abated as Jack had become a more constant visitor, and she became more familiar with his nature and aims in life. Zoe was finding out slowly that behind that showbiz personality was an ordinary soul trying to keep his feet firmly on the ground. She wondered how two cousins could be so different. They were both tall, dark, and well-built, but there the resemblance unhappily ended.

As far as she could see with Mr Unsmiling Personality, he was arrogant, thought he was a gift to the female of the species, if his cousin was to be believed, and spent most of his time with his head immersed in business. Women, it seemed, were a disposable commodity. She certainly wouldn't envy anyone that he decided to choose as his wife. Zoe frowned crossly, what on earth had made her think of marriage? She put off entering the room for as long as possible, then slipped in quietly, feeling relieved when nobody seemed to notice her. She was mistaken, Daniel knew as soon as she had entered. He was standing holding a drink, his eyes fixed on the kitchen door and let his breath out slowly as she appeared, feeling his skin prickle with awareness and his body harden in reaction.

As Zoe skirted the room, she glanced across at the big glowering man. Now what have I done? she thought, as her heartbeat accelerated wildly. She knew he liked women, so it must be her who ticked him off. For some reason, she couldn't seem to tear her gaze away from his, and heat surged up into her body at his intense stare.

Daniel pushed his way through the others as though drawn by an invisible thread and trapped her in the corner where she had sought to hide herself, his broad shoulders obscuring her view of the room. He didn't speak, merely gazed down, completely unnerving her. Zoe opened her mouth wanting to ask him to move, but her voice died away as she saw the sensuously aware glitter in his narrowed green eyes. He seemed to be fascinated by her mouth and her breath caught in her throat, as he leaned forward and then, almost as though unaware of his actions, he lowered his head and touched her lips lightly, tantalisingly, with his own. It was as though an electric current had passed between the two, making them both jerk back sharply with shock.

She gasped as his eyes darkened, and what might have happened next, if they had not been interrupted at that moment by Janine's petulant voice, was open to speculation.

"What on earth are you doing over in this dark corner, darling," she asked throatily, sliding her arm possessively through Daniel's.

Zoe came down to earth with a jolt, her heart sinking with humiliation. What had she been thinking? Had she completely lost her senses? He had been toying with her, and she had let him, like some dizzy teenager. She was furious with herself for her own stupid reaction to him and with him for thinking that he could just kiss her when he liked after his previous obnoxious behaviour. And why had he kissed her when he was obviously dating Janine? Suppose his girlfriend had not appeared, would he have kissed her again? You would have let him, a small voice whispered in her mind.

"Rubbish," Zoe muttered out loud.

She was still steaming with rage, and although she wouldn't admit it, a deep hurt, as he was led docilely away by the glamorous star. When they sat down for their meal, Zoe made sure that her seat was as far away from Daniel as the small gathering allowed. As for food, it might as well have been shredded carpet as far as she was concerned. She was doing her level best to like Janine, but it was an uphill struggle, and in the face of the other girl's complete disinterest, she gave up trying. The rest of the evening was spent in a daze, and she was relieved when it was finally over. She felt strangely deflated as they cleared up and when Libby probed about her silence, made tiredness an excuse. How could she explain her own irrational feelings to her sister, when she didn't even understand them herself?

She was not to know that Daniel had allowed Janine to tow him away because he didn't trust his own helpless response to Zoe, and heaven knows what might have happened if she hadn't removed him from temptation. Daniel had never behaved like that in his life before and he felt like a pathetic schoolboy. He could feel a noose tightening, his life being taken over. This had to stop, he must avoid her at all costs, no way must he see her again.

In Jack's hotel room later, Daniel stared at his cousin's angry face in consternation. All he had said was that it might be a good idea not to get too serious, but he hadn't bargained on Jack's growing emotional attachment to Libby.

"You hardly know her and besides, there are plenty of glamorous girls back in America only too willing to go out with you," Daniel pointed out. "You can take your pick."

"Get it through your thick head," Jack yelled angrily, "I don't want some empty-headed bimbo, I want a real girl, one who doesn't mind commitment and doesn't want her name up in bigger lights than mine."

"Commitment?" Daniel echoed in concern. How serious had this become? He felt a sense of panic as he had visions of a wedding in the offing and being permanently attached in some way to that disruptive woman. Somehow, he had to sever his cousin's ties with this family, they spelled all sorts of trouble to come. He was fighting for his life here.

Zoe allowed Libby to persuade her to go and see the release of one of Jack's earlier 'Tronicman' efforts. Despite her reservations, she found herself enjoying the light-hearted good-conquers-all story of a superhero rescuing a grateful and of course, breathtakingly beautiful maiden. The only sour note as far as Zoe was concerned was the fact that the damsel in distress was played - badly, she was pleased to note - by Janine.

As they made their way outside of the cinema afterwards, Libby quizzed her eagerly on her opinion of the film, and Zoe had to confess that she had been suitably entertained.

"All right, so I enjoyed myself, and Jack makes a terrific hero. That suit is something else," she rolled her eyes. "It doesn't leave much to the imagination, does it?"

She laughed as Libby hissed, "Hands off."

Jack was exceptionally good-looking, Zoe mused, what was not to like about the large muscular, charismatic man who played the role of superhero with such panache? Seeing him up there on screen, larger than life, brought it home to her just how much her sister's lifestyle and his differed. She began to fret about that fact, and by the time she had let herself into her flat, her mind was consumed with worry for Libby. What happened when he left for America, just where did that leave her sister, another broken-hearted girl languishing by the wayside? The two seemed very close, and she knew that her sister had crossed that threshold between casual and intimate with Jack, because the last time Libby had stayed overnight with her, she had come in very late looking flushed and dishevelled. Zoe had stared with worried eyes at her

sister's glowing face, she had looked so happy and fulfilled. It seemed that despite her reservations, the romance was still holding out.

"Hi, how did the evening go?" Zoe had called out.

"Wonderful, it's so exciting being with him." Libby's eyes shone. "I think that he really is more than fond of me."

Zoe looked at her sister with concern, she wondered how to caution her without sounding like some old busybody. She was only two years senior to her sister, yet sometimes she felt so much older than that. "How do you really feel about him, Libby?" she asked. "Apart from being impressed by his star status."

"On my part, I think it's becoming something much deeper. Nothing to do with his fame, I might add. I got over that silliness some while ago. I don't know about Jack, sometimes I catch a look that heartens me." Libby said, her eyes misty. She paused and giggled. "We're certainly compatible in all other ways."

"Oh, Lib, have you...er... Has anything...?" Zoe stared at her in growing alarm. "You know, have you been careful?"

"Yes, we did, and yes, we have," Libby laughed in amusement at her pink face. She became more serious as she saw her sister's genuine concern. "I'm not as irresponsible as I appear, Zoe. I have to really like a man to take this step, so please don't worry about me."

"It's Jack that I'm worried about." Zoe saw her sister's raised brows and hastily added. "I meant the effect that it will have on you if he takes off and doesn't come back."

"I wonder about that myself sometimes." Libby sank down slowly onto the couch. "Even you just reminding me of such a possibility makes my heart sink." She sat silently, looking sightlessly down at her folded hands, accepting the cup of coffee her sister passed her without a word. Libby suddenly looked up; her face determined. "I will enjoy it while it lasts, and perhaps it is only a passing fancy on his part. I can only hope it's more than that. If not, I shall have to live on my memories, won't I?" Libby sat and drank her coffee quickly, then made her excuses and slipped quietly into the bedroom, making it plain that she didn't wish to discuss the subject any further.

Zoe sat and stared at the closed door; she had seen the sadness in her sister's eyes as she had turned away. It seemed that Libby's feelings were much more deeply involved than she was admitting.

Chapter Three

Daniel was also aware of the escalating romance between his cousin and Libby, his anxiety increasing as time went on. It seemed that he would have to work a bit harder to break this dangerous situation up. It was easy enough to sow the seeds of doubt in Libby's mind, when he did occasionally bump into her in Jack's hotel room. A dropped hint here, an unguarded photo taken from the American papers with accompanying lurid prose on Jack's latest escapades with a selection of beautiful starlets, left where she would be sure to see it. All things that undermined Libby's confidence in her own importance in Jack's life. If Daniel's conscience pricked him at all, he justified his actions by telling himself that it was in Jack's best interests.

Zoe observed the growing conflict between her sister and Jack, his handsome face puzzled as he had to cancel dates he had arranged with friends because Libby was so insecure that she wouldn't go. Worrying about their opinions, wondering which of his female acquaintances that she was introduced to had been one of his previous girlfriends. Her incessant questioning on the photographs that appeared in the press with suspicious regularity just added fuel to the inevitable big explosion that occurred, with Jack slamming out, calling Libby small-minded and just as stupid as the vacuous starlets he disliked so much. Libby broke down and wept copiously until she had nothing left, except the occasional hiccup. Daniel had done his work exceptionally well.

Zoe commiserated with her on the unreasonable mind of men, then tentatively suggested that her sister may also have been slightly at fault. This just led to another flood of tears, and the accusation that Zoe was taking Jack's side in the argument. By the end of the week, Zoe was at her wits end. Libby had fluctuated between raging at Jack's obstinate nature and heaping the blame for the quarrel upon her own head. In the finish, Libby spent most of her time when she wasn't at work staring out of the window, her dejected figure making Zoe sigh with despair. Libby's increasing misery finally drove Zoe to go ahead with her plan to tackle Jack about the breakup. That the two were in love with each other was beyond doubt and perhaps her interference wouldn't be welcome, but there was more to this than met the eye, and she was going to find out what, even if Jack threw her out.

When Zoe entered the select hotel where Jack was staying and approached the reception desk, she felt distinctly out of place. She straightened her shoulders and pasted a confident look on her face.

"Could I please have Mr Hammell's room number?"

The receptionist, a tall, immaculately dressed young woman, looked askance at the casually dressed girl in front of her, no doubt wondering how she had the gall to even try and ask for him. "We don't give out room numbers, I'm afraid, it's against hotel policy unless the occupant stipulates otherwise. And I am sure that you must be aware of how many women have requested exactly that same much sought-after information, madame." She gave Zoe a polite empty smile and nodded towards the reporters milling around the reception area. Strangely enough, most of them appeared to be female. Any other fans were being kept at bay by the rather large doorman, and Zoe could only assume that she, herself, had been able to slip in while he was otherwise occupied.

She pulled herself up to her full height, gave her name and stared haughtily at the woman. "Well, could you please ring and tell Mr Hammell that I am here?"

"Very well, madame, I shall try." Her voice insinuated that it would be a complete waste of time. While she rang, the receptionist kept her eye fixed firmly on Zoe, as though she expected her to make a bolt for the elevator or stairs. Now that's a thought, Zoe mused, then spotted the burly man in uniform standing by the lift doors keeping a keen eye on proceedings. Not such a good idea.

The girl's expression underwent a metamorphosis as she put the phone down and gave a practised if stunned smile. "Mr Hammell will see you now," she said, trying to keep the surprise out of her voice. "If you would care to go up."

She gave Zoe his room number and nodded across at the gimlet-eyed man, who watched suspiciously as Zoe approached the elevator. He opened the doors, glancing quickly around and ushered her in, leaving a lot of speculative eyes watching her preferential treatment. Zoe felt as though she were in a spy movie and giggled to herself, so this was what a film star had to tolerate. She stood in the elevator, going over in her mind as to what to say to the angry and hurt young man. How would Jack react to her interference? Perhaps she was pushing Libby onto him, and maybe it had been his way of ending the relationship. No, she couldn't accept that. Jack had been genuinely upset when he'd left. No one could have put that much emotion into the parting scene, no matter how good an actor.

When she stepped out of the elevator, Zoe was taken aback, as she approached his door, to see two large security men standing on either side. A necessity, she supposed, but she still felt like a groupie as she neared them, and they both gazed at her with world-weary expressions. She mumbled her name with a red face and one of them tapped on the door. She needn't have worried about Jack's reaction to seeing her, his haggard face lit up when he saw her, and the unhappiness in his eyes made her heart go out to him.

"Do you always have those watchdogs at the door?" she asked lightly.

"Oh, yeah. Welcome to the weird world of the slightly deranged, and enter my prison." He gave her a brief smile and turning away, threw himself down into a plush armchair, saying despondently. "It's no use, Zoe; she won't trust me, and I can't go on listening to her endlessly accusing me of affairs. I would need to be on drugs to keep up with all the women that I'm supposed to have gone out with, and no, I do not do drugs, so you can take that worried look off your face."

"Sorry, Jack, but we hear so much about that kind of thing in the media, and you can't blame me for wondering." She sat herself down on the seat opposite him and paused, searching for the right words. "Libby is so upset and miserable over this quarrel. Have you not wondered what started her off on all this? She knew the kind of world that you move in, and she accepted that. Now suddenly she's watching your every move and continually questioning you. I know my sister, there's normally not a jealous bone in her body, unless something or someone has undermined her confidence and planted serious doubts."

"Daniel said it would probably turn out like this, but who would...?" Jack said, puzzled. His voice trailed off as the same unpleasant thought entered both minds simultaneously. "Damn!" Jack jerked upright. "The only one with the opportunity or crafty enough is Daniel, the rotten swine. But why?"

"Because we're not quite what he would wish for your family, I suppose," Zoe fumed, "not good enough for Mr High and Mighty."

"Daniel isn't a snob, Zoe, whatever else he may be," Jack said. "A devious bastard, yes, that he can certainly be. Perhaps he was just protecting me. Maybe he thinks that Libby isn't really serious about us?"

"That's a lot of trouble to go to if she just thinks that way," Zoe snorted, "If such was the case, Libby would just get fed up and leave you, wouldn't she?"

"Not necessarily, some might think that she would stay for the prestige and money." He held his hands up placatingly at her angry face.

"I don't mean me, just speculating on how it might look to someone else."

"Meaning that loathsome cousin of yours, I suppose." Zoe sat with her fingernails sinking into the soft arm of the chair, wishing that it was Daniel's throat.

"Do you think that Libby will see me," Jack asked sadly, "after all the stupid remarks I threw at her?"

"She was equally at fault," said Zoe, remembering the hurtful words that her sister had flung like stones at him. "I should imagine she'll be so pleased to see you that you won't be wasting much time on talking."

She laughed as he gathered his jacket up, snatched his car keys off the table and marched her quickly to the door. "We're wasting precious time," he said impatiently. "Let's go."

"How serious are you, Jack?" Zoe put her hand on the door to prevent him from opening it. She sought for the right words, not wanting to trap him into making false promises. Zoe stared at him probingly. "If this is just a romantic fling, wouldn't it be wiser to leave things as they are? Don't break her heart and carry this on if it means nothing to you."

"I can appreciate that you've got her best interests at heart," Jack said, trying to hold on to his frayed temper. He shut his eyes tiredly, "I just wish, for once, someone would give me credit for some finer feelings. We actors are not all shallow, you know!"

"I'm sorry, Jack," Zoe put her hand on his arm, "but I can't help worrying about Libby. She's important to me."

"Yeah, well, let me assure you that it's serious," he smiled earnestly at her, "at least on my part." He looked searchingly at her, wanting reassurance about the depth of Libby's feelings.

"I can only say that she's more upset about this than I've ever seen her," Zoe consoled him. "As to her inner emotions, you'll have to find that out for yourself, but tell her how you really feel."

"It makes me so mad," he groaned with annoyance as they entered the elevator. "I have to leave first thing in the morning to film on location in the Grand Canyon, and I wanted to have this out with that conniving cousin of mine. The nuisance of it is that he's over in Canada now on business and won't be back for two weeks."

"Why did he go away when he knew you were leaving for the States in the morning?" she asked. "Doesn't he see you off, a fond farewell and all that?"

"Not usually," he shrugged, "Why would he? I have to fly off at a moment's notice with filming and he has the same problem in his business. You get used to it. We do keep in touch, sometimes he comes over and stays in my pad and I visit him at his house now and then, we meet up whenever we get the chance."

"What line of business is he in?" Zoe was curious to know what kept the large morose man so busy.

"Oh, some computer software business, I think," he said vaguely.

Before she could probe further, the elevator doors opened, and she was confronted by a vast, dark parking lot. "Where are we?" Zoe asked, running to keep up with Jack's long stride.

"Basement car park," he said, making his way to a small beaten-up-looking car with darkened windows. "Like my cunning disguise?"

"Very well camouflaged," she laughed as she looked over the battered vehicle at him. "I didn't know it was a car until you pointed it out."

As Jack drove her home, Zoe sat in his car listening to him grumble frustratedly about not being able to tackle Daniel on the deliberate misunderstanding he had caused between Libby and himself.

"Hmm, leave that man to me," Zoe said thoughtfully with an angry glint in her eye, which made him laugh out loud.

"What are you planning," he chuckled, "something excruciatingly painful?"

Jack stared at the determined expression on her face with glee. If that look was anything to go by, his cousin was going to pay dearly for his unwanted interference. When they reached her flat, Zoe quickly made herself scarce, leaving the couple to resolve their differences. She ventured down from her studio two hours later to find them on the couch as closely entwined as decency permitted, given the fact that Zoe could have walked in on them at any time. With the problem between the two young people sorted out and Jack promising to come back as soon as possible, Zoe got Daniel's London address and the place where he worked, from Jack before he left.

ＵＵＵＵＵＵＵ

Zoe set out her plan of campaign, nothing drastic, just a short visit to his office, a little loud embarrassment to start with, she decided, perhaps rest for a day or two, and then another sneak attack. The only problem about attacking such a large fortress was that your own army had to be as formidable as the enemy's and Zoe hadn't taken this into account, as she would soon find out.

She chose the day after Daniel had returned from his trip. He probably thought that he was going to have some peace and quiet. Well, she had news for him. When she arrived at his office, she was taken aback as she gazed up at the sheer size of the place, her heart hammering at her own audacity. The brass plaque on the outside of the building made her hesitate, as she realised that the whole block belonged to the Hammell Group and Zoe began to wonder if her plan was such a good idea. She nearly turned tail and fled, but was spurred on by the thought of Daniel's arrogant assumption of Libby not being a suitable girl for his cousin to be taking out, and her anger carried her forward into the entrance hall.

"Can I help you?" the young man behind the highly polished desk inquired politely.

One could hardly call it a desk; it was almost intimidating. The gleaming wood ran the length of one wall in the massive entrance hall and was manned by several efficient looking staff, who were dealing with a constant flow of immaculately dressed businesspeople.

Zoe cleared her throat, trying to inject a note of confidence into her voice. "Yes," she said, smiling across at his friendly face. "Could you tell me which floor Mr Hammell's office is situated on, please?"

"Mr Hammell?" His eyes rounded in surprise. His boss was a strictly appointment-only man. Usually, people who were expected just walked up to his floor and were screened up there.

Zoe's lips tightened in vexation at the man's struck expression. You would think that she'd asked if God were in. "Yes," she said patiently, "Mr Daniel Hammell, he asked me to call in on him today."

He gave her the required information, knowing full well that if she wasn't expected by his boss, she would be given short shrift and shown the door by Mr Hammell's very efficient secretary. He directed her to the right elevator and watched her with interested eyes until she disappeared from sight, wondering if she was anybody he should know.

As Zoe entered the elevator, she began to get cold feet again and had to remind herself precisely why she was there. It was to tackle the beast in his lair, and it was for Libby. Standing outside his office, she rubbed her moist hands nervously down her skirt several times, before gathering her courage together. Tossing her hair and lifting her chin, Zoe swept in, striding imperiously up to the secretary's desk.

"Could you please inform Mr Hammell that Zoe Burgess is here to see him?"

The secretary slowly sat back and adjusted her glasses to peer up at this slightly flushed, attractive young woman trying so hard to look cool and poised. "Have you an appointment with Mr Hammell?" she enquired politely, her voice cool. This was not the first woman that she'd had the occasion to see off. In fact, it was becoming quite a nuisance. Her boss was a very imposing and handsome man, the fact that Jack being his cousin enhanced his charms was something that

Daniel was very aware of and had cause to rue, so she did her level best to try and vet very carefully any woman who came seeking him.

Zoe stared at the middle-aged woman, who was regarding her with a stony face. “No, I’m sorry, I don’t have an appointment, but I did promise to call when I was next in town.” She tried a friendly smile, which appeared to cut no ice with the stern-faced woman.

“I will inform him that you’re here, but I have to warn you that he is a very busy man,” the secretary stated firmly.

“I’m sure that he’ll make time to see me,” Zoe said in a determined voice.

The woman gave her a jaundiced look and buzzed through to the larger office behind her, to announce his visitor, knowing that Daniel was in conference with his colleagues at the moment and she fully expected him to refuse to see this young woman. She was therefore visibly startled when his deep voice said abruptly, “Tell her to wait.” She turned to Zoe. “Could you please take a seat, Miss Burgess, it shouldn’t be too long.” Her face was a bit more friendly now but still reserved. “He’s in a meeting at the moment. Do help yourself to a magazine while you wait.”

An hour passed and still Daniel had made no move to call her in. Zoe had worked her way through all the magazines on offer and was fuming. How dare he leave her to stew like this? She was convinced that he was doing it deliberately, his guilty conscience prodding him, no doubt, hoping that she would give up and go away.

“That’s it,” Zoe muttered as she jumped to her feet, taking the secretary by surprise. She strode over to the door, ignoring the faint protest that the woman uttered, and shoved it open with enough force to make it crack against the wall. She nearly turned tail as she was confronted by a group of men, shirt sleeves rolled up, seated at a large rectangular table. Briefcases were open, papers strewn across the surface and all were regarding her with the same shocked expression on their faces. Except Daniel, who was watching her with a thunderous frown furrowing his dark brow.

"Could you please wait outside until I have finished in here," he said icily. She hesitated, but the supercilious lift of his brows as he looked back at the other men inflamed her already short temper.

"No! I cannot wait, I have sat out there for over an hour doing just that, you thoroughly obnoxious man, and by the way, your magazines really do need updating. People will forget which century they're in if they are left sitting in your waiting room for too long," Zoe snapped. "Talk to me now, tell me why you interfered in Jack's affairs."

"Not here, I think," Daniel snarled, in a low voice, "this is better discussed in private."

"I don't want to be anywhere alone with you if I can help it," she stated, "You...you reptile."

Daniel's brows shot up at her belligerent attitude and he leaned back in his chair looking at Zoe with a faint sneering curl of his lips, which only served to make her temper escalate.

"Control yourself, woman, and stop making such a spectacle of yourself," he drawled contemptuously.

That did it, and Zoe rushed forward, thumping the desk with her small fist, raising a few smiles on the other men's faces. She looked across at him and her rage was such that she was totally oblivious of the others as she put her hands flat on the table and leaned across, glaring at him, wishing that she could thump him squarely on his large arrogant nose.

Daniel just sat and regarded her with a set angry expression, feeling trapped and also, to his chagrin, strangely excited by the virago confronting him.

"Do you even know or care what you've put Libby and Jack through?" Zoe hissed, leaning closer. "You are a pompous, self-opinionated, insufferable prig. Be a miserable despot if you want to, but leave Jack to find his own salvation. Don't drag other people down into your pit of despondency with you."

The secretary hovering outside of the door was left in no doubt that this was not one of the usual simpering women who plagued him. In fact, she sounded as though she might just kill him.

Daniel's face had suffused with colour at her insults, and as he became aware of the other men's smothered laughter, his temper exploded. They had never seen him so flustered before and it was an eye-opener. He nearly knocked his chair over in his haste to get up and marching around the table with barely leashed fury, grabbed her arm and hustled her towards the door.

"Unhand me, you beast!" she yelled, sounding like something from a Victorian melodrama.

"Allow me to know what is best for my cousin, you interfering pest. Now, obviously, I shall have to assist you to leave," he growled down at her, trying to keep his voice down to a dull roar. "It's no good requesting that you do so, because you wouldn't know politeness if it reared up and bit you."

As they reached the entrance, Zoe wrenched her arm away, making him lose his balance and he tripped on the expensive rug that lay across the polished floor. He fell to his knees at her feet, his head pressed against the top of her legs.

Just when he thought things couldn't get any worse, Zoe leaned down and said loudly, with malicious relish, "Oh! Please, Daniel, we hardly know each other." She gazed at him dreamily and simpered, "And that was very wicked of you. You mustn't whisper such things. Although if you wish to explore that suggestion, I'm more than willing."

She gave him a provocative smile and kissed his forehead in full view of the other men, making a quick but dignified exit, leaving him brimming with rage and something he would rather not explore, to face the roomful of grinning men.

That would teach him, she fumed; his colleagues had been unable to hear their muttered exchange until she had raised her voice. I hope they think that he was propositioning me, the beast.

Daniel felt as though he had been branded where her lips had touched. He was sure there was a hole burnt in his head. He even put his hand up to check. Standing up, he brushed his trousers down, trying to regain a semblance of cool dignity. How dare she embarrass him in front of his colleagues like this? That he might have been the initial cause of such a scene, he summarily dismissed. He walked stiffly back to his chair, his face flushed, and sat down outwardly calm, but for the first time in his life, he could no longer concentrate on the ideas being bandied about around the table. So, he sat with his hands tightly clasped, a look of polite interest on his face, apparently listening to the flow of conversation, but inside he was going through various scenarios on how he would exact his revenge on that bloody awful woman. To think that he had actually felt attracted to her. Well, he'd had a lucky escape, hadn't he? Imagine going out with that bundle of trouble...imagine!

Daniel shook himself angrily as his mind dwelt on her and not with revenge in mind. This wouldn't do, he was going to pieces, this woman was positively lethal. As he brooded, he became aware of a persistent voice beside him. "Sir, what do you say, do you think that it's a viable proposition?"

Daniel looked blankly at the speaker, then sat up and cleared his throat. "Sorry, gentlemen, I seem to have lost track of the plot, do you mind if we take a break for half an hour?" He stood up, making it an order, and stalked from the room.

"Well, well," one of the men drawled, as the door shut behind him, "she's certainly got under his skin."

The other men laughed as they relaxed and helped themselves to coffee, welcoming this unexpected break.

Daniel could hear the muffled laughter even through the solid wood of the door and gnashed his teeth impotently. He suspected that the humour was at his own expense, and it was one more black mark against her. He would get his own back, even if he died in the attempt.

His secretary bit her lip to stop the smile that threatened. She had never seen him lose his calm demeanour before, not like this, but then to her knowledge nobody had ever spoken to him like that either. He was always such a commanding figure, so confident. He would be horrified if he could see how he appeared to her at this moment. She glanced across at him surreptitiously. He was standing staring out of the window with a faint flush of anger on his rugged face, breathing heavily, his hands clenching and flexing as though he would like to strangle someone.

Zoe hastened out of the elevator and exited the building as though she feared for her life, and that's exactly how she was feeling. When she had leaned close to Daniel, for a moment her mind had whirled at the sheer masculine presence of the man. His strong muscular arms displayed by his rolled-up shirt sleeves had an unnerving effect upon her, and where his buttons had been undone exposing his broad chest, Zoe had felt the heat of his body and had been very tempted to reach out and touch him. The most annoying part was that when his head had been pressed against her legs, she'd had a terrible time suppressing the urge to hold him there and was horrified by her own idiotic behaviour, wondering just what she would have done had they been alone. She wasn't sure who had come off worst in that encounter, but she would be very careful from now on to avoid him at all costs.

Daniel stood looking down on the street below, watching fixedly as he saw her small figure crossing the road. She was an absolute pain in the backside, and she'd had the gall to come barging in here and lecture him about the handling of his own cousin. He glared angrily at her, lifting his hand slowly, encompassing her image in it as though he would crush her and then imagined trapping her in his arms. The thought of touching her anywhere filled him with a sense of excitement and he dropped his hand abruptly. Daniel was thoroughly disgusted with himself for this sign of weakness, but he couldn't get her out of his mind. Every time he thought of her, his blood pressure rose and that's not all, she had a strangely painful effect on his libido. As he became aware of his secretary's scrutiny, he swung around.

"Haven't you got any work to do?" he snapped, glowering at her.

She jumped and frowned at him over the top of her glasses. "As you will observe," his secretary said crisply, "I'm attending to it as we speak, Mr Hammel."

Daniel ran his hand agitatedly through his hair and sighed. "I apologise, Margaret, take no notice of my bad manners," he smiled wearily at her, "I really am sorry, I don't know what's wrong with me today, apart from that darned silly woman interrupting our meeting."

Margaret smiled to herself and waved her hand airily. "Don't worry about it, you're probably just tired, sir." She stared up at him sympathetically. "You only arrived back from Canada yesterday. I expect the flight is catching up with you."

"Yes, you're probably right, it was a tiring two weeks." He looked as though she had thrown him a lifeline. What with the journey and being harangued in his own office, he was bound to feel undone.

He walked back into his office feeling relieved. That must be it. Losing control of his temper like this was something that he rarely did, he probably just needed a rest. This fact was brought home to him when he had returned to the room and resumed the meeting, because he was so preoccupied that Daniel didn't hear the question that one of his colleagues fired at him. This was the second time he'd had a lapse of concentration, and it wouldn't do.

"No," Daniel muttered, as he stood up abruptly. The men stared at him in amazement as he left them without a word and stalked to the door. One of the younger men followed him.

"Is there a problem, Daniel, can I be of help in some way?"

"No!" Daniel snapped as he was jolted out of his private world, then in a more conciliatory tone, "No, I can't possibly delegate on this one, this is one task I have to deal with myself." He glanced back as he became aware of the waiting silence in the room behind him, feeling obliged to offer them some sort of explanation. "Sorry, gentlemen, a thorny problem has cropped up. I have to deal with it immediately."

The men looked at him and then each other. It must be important to make him walk out on this discussion. They may not have been so impressed if they had seen the rattled man who made his way wearily home and poured himself a stiff drink the moment he got in, throwing it back in one desperate gulp.

The young man clearing the papers at the end of the meeting glanced down at his boss's notepad and stared at it with puzzled eyes. There were no comments jotted down as there would normally have been about the various ideas put forward. Instead there was a woman's name scrawled all over the page. Who on earth was Zoe? He paused thoughtfully and a slow smile lit his face as he remembered the distracting little scene that had taken place earlier. "Don't tell me the boss has been hooked at last," he murmured, this was too good to be kept to himself.

ꕤꕤꕤꕤꕤꕤꕤ

Zoe slumped down at her kitchen table, her head propped up on one hand, sipping coffee, not that she could taste it. Her head ached and her heart thumped with anxiety at her own appalling antics. How could she have behaved in such a way? She, who was normally so reserved. She had wanted to embarrass him, but in a calm controlled manner, not screech across the desk like some ill-mannered harpy, and whatever had possessed her to think that she could possibly make any difference to how Daniel thought? If anything, it would simply confirm his low opinion of her and Libby. Those poor men probably thought that she came straight out of a nightmare, something that you kept chained in your attic, she thought with a groan. For some reason that man possessed the power to make her become almost demented, causing her to behave in a horribly childish way. She touched her lips, certain that they were swollen through contact with his skin. That's it, she was allergic to him.

It took several days for Zoe to stop worrying about her mental aberration, and then she began to relax. Although Daniel's face haunted her at night, making her toss and turn restlessly, she was learning to push him to the back of her mind. At least her sister had reason to be happy now. Jack had phoned Libby every day, had flown back twice to see her, and would be doing so again at the weekend. The couple had now decided to discuss everything that worried them, be more open with each other in the future and woe betide Daniel if he ever interfered again.

Zoe was visiting with Libby and Jack had flown over again as promised. He was telling them about his recent decision to leave show business.

"Why now," Zoe asked him, "when your films are so popular?"

Jack sat on the sofa next to Libby, leaning forward, his face in his hands, rubbing his face tiredly, and said in a muffled voice, "For one thing, I'm sick and tired of wearing ridiculous blonde wigs and a stupid moustache just to walk unrecognised into my own hotel. I don't know why I bother anyway; they always seem to see straight through my cunning disguise." He dropped his hands and grinned wryly. "As my cousin is constantly pointing out, fame is fleeting, and I'm no great actor."

"Nonsense, Jack, I enjoyed your performance in Tronicman. I don't know anyone else who could play it so well," Zoe butted in, adding with a frown, "Trust that man to say something so incredibly nasty."

"Pure entertainment, not great acting, and Daniel is right," he smiled. "My other reason is that if I want to get married and keep my wife happy and wealthy, I have to explore other avenues to be sure of survival." He put his arm around Libby's shoulders, giving her an affectionate hug as she leaned against him.

"Oh, Jack, you don't need to earn a fortune to keep me," she said, chastising him gently and gazing up at him lovingly. "We wouldn't starve, I have a good job, one that I love, and I don't mind working for as long as it takes you to make a fresh start if that's what you really want to do."

Jack hugged her, at a loss for words, making Zoe's heart melt as he looked down at Libby with such love in his eyes. It was plain to see he thought the world of her sister. She was content in the knowledge that no matter what happened in the future, at this moment in time, they were more than happy to be together.

Chapter Four

Zoe was tired and listless, she had stayed late at work to complete a special rush order, as a favour to her boss. Now she was so hungry that she couldn't wait until she got home, so she went into the small newly-established bar near to her workplace. Her boss had suggested that she might try it. Apparently, the person who placed the late order had recommended the place to him only that day.

The bar had a nice cosy atmosphere, the people were friendly, and the food smelled appetising.

Zoe ordered a coffee and a sandwich, seating herself at a small table in the corner, relaxing as she listened to the buzz of conversation around her. She swallowed her drink in record time, it had been thirsty work concentrating on the designs the client had asked for, and she wondered why he had required so many. She shrugged, munching gratefully on her sandwich, hoping that the sound of her rumbling stomach wasn't attracting too much attention, and ordered another coffee. She glanced up idly as she sipped her drink, nearly choking as she saw Daniel entering the door, carrying a large bunch of flowers, and beaming menacingly as he strode towards her.

"Darling," he bellowed, "I'm totally lost for words, last night was out of this world. Just wonderful."

"What do you mean?" She sat rigidly, gazing up at him warily. "Why was last night wonderful?"

He threw back his head and laughed aloud, as though she were being extremely witty. "You little tease." Daniel's eyes glittered maliciously at her. "We had a really good time though, didn't we? Something we will have to repeat, it was so unforgettable."

"Will you please lower your voice," Zoe said through gritted teeth. For someone who was supposed to be lost for words, he was certainly spouting quite a few, she thought angrily. "I'm sure that the people in here don't want to share in your inane remarks."

Daniel's voice remained at the same resounding level as he carried on. "I could tell that you weren't disappointed," he smiled modestly, and sighed reminiscently "Whew, that thing you do with your hands...well, words fail me. Wow!"

Zoe froze with embarrassment as some of the intrigued spectators began to snigger. "I don't know who this man is," she said loudly, "If you don't go away, I shall call the manager."

"How could you pretend not to know me," Daniel said, his face stricken as he sank down into the seat opposite hers. "Or am I just another face among your many conquests? Did last night mean nothing to you? Here was I thinking that there was something special between us."

A tide of hot colour rose to her hairline, and she felt as though her whole body had stiffened with the horror of the situation. As Zoe glared at him, she saw the gleam of satisfaction in his eyes and felt her fingers curl, wanting to clamp them to his throat.

"Got you," Daniel whispered softly, as he leaned towards her. "How does it feel, to be the centre of all this attention?"

She looked around at all the staring eyes with appalled outrage, and hastily averted her eyes. "I'm not particularly bothered," she managed to get out, trying to look as though being the focus of everyone's undivided interest wasn't troubling her one iota.

"Oh, dear," Daniel smiled nastily, "not the right answer, I'm afraid." He leaned his arms on the table and sighed gustily. "You made me such promises," he said in a hurt voice, looking sorrowfully at the two women sitting at the nearby table, and giving them a sad smile.

One of them gave Zoe an admonishing frown, the other tut-tutted. In fact, she could feel the whole bar beginning to hum with disapproval. "Will you please go away." She lowered her voice to a faint whisper. "You don't want me coming back your office again, do you, making you squirm?"

"There you go again," he heaved a despondent sigh, "making promises."

"I did no such thing!" Zoe hissed, her face flaming. "Please be quiet."

"Then don't ever try and lecture or embarrass me in front of my staff and colleagues again." he warned softly, narrowing his eyes. "I make a very formidable enemy, so don't ever antagonise me."

"Is this the best you can do," she sneered, then wished she hadn't. The menacing smile he gave her made goosebumps rise up on her scalp.

"Are you by any chance challenging me?" Daniel enquired politely, his tone threatening. "I too can cause havoc. Now let me see, where is it that you work?"

"You wouldn't dare," she breathed in horror.

"Wouldn't dare," he repeated, savouring the words, and raising his brows. "Are you perhaps goading me into taking you up on it?"

"No! Will you stop this?" Zoe said, near to tears. "Leave me alone."

"Willingly." Daniel glared at her, pushing his chair back as he stood up. "I think that we understand each other perfectly now."

"You bet we do," she said angrily, her throat tight with humiliation. "Let's hope we never have the misfortune to see each other again."

"I second that." He looked down at her, his eyes glinting with anger. "Perhaps you'll think twice before you try and make a fool of me again."

"You're easy to make a fool of," Zoe said nastily, not able to resist the barb.

"Hmm, not quite taken due warning yet, I see. Enjoy your late order, did you?" Daniel stared at her, his green eyes like polished flint and smiled maliciously at the dawning realisation on her face; that he was the client responsible for her working so hard and late. He obviously had no intention of actually paying for the time and effort she had put in.

"You rotten beast," she gasped.

"I told you," Daniel reminded her, "Don't cross me if you cannot cope with the consequences."

Zoe stared at him, her mouth opening to retaliate against this overbearing man, but words deserted her as she saw his hostile expression.

"No cutting reply?" he mocked.

"Oh, go away," she said in a tired voice. For some reason, the thought that he was only too pleased not to have to see her again made her feel incredibly depressed.

Daniel hesitated as he watched her downcast head and instead of feeling triumphant, he felt like a complete heel. "Are you okay?"

She didn't answer, she couldn't, she was afraid to even look at him.

"Look at me." He sank down into the seat again, put his hand under her chin and lifted her face gently. "Oh, God," he groaned, as he saw her tear-filled eyes. "Don't cry, I didn't mean to make you cry."

"I am *not* crying," she gulped, dabbing at her face. "Someone like you couldn't make me cry in a million years." Her voice ended in an undignified sob, and she pressed a tissue to her brimming eyes, wishing that he would go away. The people taking such an avid interest in these proceedings probably thought that she deserved all she got, and if she were honest, perhaps she did. Her actions had rebounded on her with a vengeance.

"Hmm, so you usually cry over your meals like this, do you?" Daniel enquired, inspecting her sandwich closely. "Yes, I can see how it would upset you. Not very appetising, is it?"

Zoe couldn't help the faint sighing laugh that escaped her at his serious expression as he studied her food so intently.

"You see, I can make you laugh, too," he said softly and gave her a half smile. "Let me take you home, it's the least I can do."

She stared across at him, wanting to say yes, yet knowing that she should say no, not quite trusting his intentions, so she just moved her head indecisively.

"Is that a yes, or no?" he asked her. "I'm the enemy, is that it, not to be trusted? Come on, let's call a brief truce while I get you safely home."

Zoe allowed herself to be guided from the bar, feeling fragile and unhappy as he helped her into his car. She couldn't imagine what had possessed her to even think of letting Daniel take her home, they seemed to strike sparks off each other, and she must remember Janine.

"I must be mad," she muttered, glancing sideways at him, watching his strong hands on the steering wheel.

"That makes two of us," he said quietly, "you drive me to distraction."

Zoe felt hot as Daniel turned his head and she saw the desire that he couldn't hide in his gleaming eyes.

"Oh, no," she protested, "don't even think in those terms. You don't even really like me."

"No, I don't like you." Daniel gave a gruff laugh. "That doesn't even begin to describe how I feel."

She hunched down in her seat, suddenly aware of how isolated she was in the car, so close to him. She was surprised and apprehensive when he stopped and then realised that they were outside her apartment already.

"Thank you for the lift," she said politely.

"I'll walk you to your door," Daniel said firmly as he undid his seat belt.

"I would rather you didn't," Zoe whispered. She didn't want this overwhelming man getting her alone. In her vulnerable state, she didn't trust her own responses. She hurriedly jumped out of the car and rushed across to the entrance of the flats.

Daniel totally ignored her order, and striding after her, followed her up the stairs, standing over her as she fumbled unsuccessfully for her key.

"Please go, Daniel," she pleaded, "I'm perfectly fine now."

"I want to be sure that you've forgiven me for making you cry."

"I told you before," she mumbled, "you didn't make me cry."

"Upset you, then," he said.

"No, you didn't," she insisted.

"You are the most argumentative woman I have ever met," Daniel rasped, "I don't know why I even bother with you."

"Nor do I," Zoe snapped, "so why don't you go away and leave me alone."

"I'm not quite sure," he said slowly, staring down at her small angry face. "I just know that I would find it hard to endure not being able to see you again."

Her lips parted in surprise at his words and a strange feeling of elation filled her. "Same here," she said softly, as she stared up into his mesmerising green eyes. "It must be a love/hate thing."

"Well, we've gone through the hate bit." His lips curled into a sensual smile. "Perhaps we should try out the love part."

"I don't think that would be a very sensible idea." She backed away from him nervously as he moved nearer. "We might make the whole situation worse."

Daniel leaned over her, one hand resting against the door above her head, the other lightly touching her arm, with such longing in his eyes that she nearly weakened.

"Let me come in," he said huskily.

"No, I can't, Daniel," she protested, knowing that her own willpower was weakened by his close proximity and that was just outside of her apartment. What would happen if she were foolish enough to let him in? "Please go home."

As she spoke, with perfect timing Libby came bounding upstairs closely followed by Jack.

"Hi, you two," she greeted cheerfully, completely blind to the charged atmosphere between the couple standing pressed against the door. "Come in, Daniel, and have coffee. You might as well, Jack is staying."

Zoe could have throttled her. Was she to have no privacy? She needed desperately to be alone with her thoughts. Libby was staying more and more often these days and was starting to treat the place as home.

As Libby turned the key, their attention was distracted by the clatter of heels on the stairs and Zoe felt drained as Janine rounded the bannisters, smiling sweetly up at Daniel. She felt like screaming. This was rapidly turning into a farce, and where had her brain been hibernating to have forgotten Janice even for one moment.

"Darling, I nearly missed you," the actress simpered. She showed her perfect teeth in a winning smile. "I didn't realise that we were to meet here."

"We weren't supposed to meet anywhere," Daniel snapped. "This is a private affair. How did you know where I would be?"

"Oh, darling," she giggled, "I simply followed Jack."

Zoe glared at him; what did he mean 'private affair'? She immediately turned to Janine with a polite smile. "Oh, please do come in, everyone else has."

As they entered the flat, Zoe went straight towards her bedroom, giving Libby a fulminating look, "No coffee for me, thanks. I'm too tired and there's plenty of company. Five's a crowd, and all that."

"Very sensible," Janine approved, as she sat down and made herself at home.

"Well, goodnight, all," Zoe said, looking straight at Daniel, her anger obvious. "Have fun."

How dare he make a play for her, when he had Janine at his beck and call. She threw herself onto her bed and punched her pillow, as if it were his head. This stupid behaviour wouldn't do, why couldn't she just respond to him in a nice friendly fashion, turn his advances away with a nonchalant laugh? At work, she had occasions to do just that when men had tried to date her, and she was still on good terms with most of them, so what was different about Daniel?

She tried to analyse her own feelings. True, he was a very attractive man, but so were plenty of others who she met, yet they'd never affected her in the same manner. If she were honest with herself, Zoe had to confess that when he came anyway near, she was consumed with desire, accompanied by a strange emotion that weakened her defences. She didn't love him, did she? How could she, he was nearly a stranger. He was the last type of man that she would choose to give her heart to, so it couldn't possibly be such a deep emotion. He was arrogant, she punched her pillow again, vain, one more punch, and if he thought that he was going to add her to his unfortunate string of women, he was very much mistaken. She threw the pillow on the floor in disgust and turned face down, lying rigid, unable to relax. It was like laying on a bed of stones.

It was nearly an hour later before she heard the front door close. A tentative knock at the bedroom door heralded Libby, as she peered across at her sister's huddled form on the bed.

"Trouble sleeping?" she enquired. "Did we disturb you too much?"

"Why do you even bother to knock if you're going to barge straight in anyway?" Zoe asked crossly. "Remind me who owns this place? I might have to change the locks."

"Don't be so crabby. You know I can pick locks anyway, so don't bother," Libby tittered. "What have you done to Daniel?"

"What do you mean, what have I done?" Zoe snapped, wriggling around onto her back and frowning at her sister. "Wasn't he content with just one woman to entertain him?"

"He was so miserable; it's a wonder Janine stayed." Libby laughed. She sat down on the edge of the bed and shook her head. "Mind you, she's so thick, I don't think that she even noticed. In fact, she did most of the talking. Zoe, he really is attracted to you, why do you push him away?"

"So attracted that he had to take Janine home?" Zoe sat up and looked at her sister knowingly. "Go on, tell me that I'm wrong."

"No," Libby said slowly, not able to argue the point. "Daniel did take her home. She made him feel so awkward that he felt obliged to."

"I rest my case." Zoe slumped back onto her pillows. "Can you honestly tell me that he leaves her at the door, a glamorous woman like that."

"I honestly don't know," her sister grimaced, "I really don't. I do know that he's got a thing about you, though."

"Not good enough," Zoe said sadly, "I don't share. I can't say that I like Janine, but it must be awful knowing that he pursues other women, so hurtful."

After that little confrontation, Zoe grilled her sister thoroughly every time she called to say she was coming over, making sure that she wouldn't try and arrange a meeting with Daniel. She wasn't safe to be left alone with him, and it wasn't Daniel's behaviour that she was worried about. She was seriously starting to worry about her own behaviour where that man was concerned. Unfortunately, her mind gave her no help whatsoever, constantly dwelling on him, disrupting her nights, filling her days, making her despair at her own weakness.

On one of her visits to Tom's flat, Zoe was pleased to bump into Chris, one of her brother's work colleagues and someone they had practically grown up with. He was such an affable and charming man that she always felt completely at ease with him, talking with him animatedly and chuckling as he reminisced about their childhood antics. She knew that at one time he had harboured a romantic attachment for her, but fortunately he had outgrown his crush, and they had remained firm friends. They left together, laughing as they ran down the stairs arm in arm, coming to an abrupt halt as their way was barred by the two large figures climbing up towards them.

"Hi!" Jack beamed, pleased to see her.

"Oh, hello, Jack, what a pity that we're just leaving," she said breathlessly, trying not to stare at the dark glowering man standing menacingly beside him.

"Must you go?" Jack asked. "Come back and join us."

"No, really," Zoe laughed lightly, "Chris and I must be off, we have a table booked." She didn't dare venture a glance at Chris and just hoped that he was masking his surprise.

Daniel brows drew together in a frown as his eyes focused on her arm tightly entwined with the handsome young man's, and he felt a fiery rage consume him. "Don't feel that you have to leave on my account," he growled aggressively.

"We were already leaving," Zoe pointed out, pulling at her friend's arm and moving quickly past them, making sure that she didn't brush against Daniel in the process, calling back over her shoulder, "Goodbye, Jack, nice to have seen you."

Once outside, she let Chris's arm drop and gave an apologetic laugh as she relaxed.

"I have never raced downstairs so fast in my life,' he chuckled.

"Sorry about that, do you mind?" Zoe asked anxiously.

"Not at all," he smiled. "I gather that you're trying to avoid the large one, carved out of granite."

Zoe couldn't help but laugh at this apt description of Daniel. "You guessed right," she giggled. "Did I bruise your arm?"

"No, just a few nail marks," he joked. "What are a few puncture holes between friends."

"I really am sorry, Chris," She rubbed at his arm. "I must be stronger than I look."

Something made her glance up at Tom's window, and she trembled as she saw Daniel staring intently down at them. He reminded her of an animal stalking its prey and her hand dropped away from Chris instinctively, as though aware that she was putting him in danger. Her own response almost took her breath away. Something inside had instantly recognised that look, a wild untamed side that was fighting to get out. Now she was really worried. How do you fight yourself; she wondered.

"Come on," she said with a shiver, as she turned away from that ferocious gaze. "Let's go. I expect you'll be wanting to get home to that beautiful wife of yours."

"Yes, I am a little late," Chris smiled, "although these wounds will take some explaining."

"Oh, dear," she said in mock alarm. She knew his wife, Laura, very well; she would find it all very amusing and would probably call her later to find out all the juicy details about this mysterious man her husband had been used as a shield against.

Daniel felt frustrated and angry. One minute he seemed to be making headway with Zoe, the next he was pushed out in the cold. What was he supposed to have done now? His conscience prodded him, and he had to admit that maybe he was guilty of a little interference, but nothing that merited this sort of treatment. She had obviously made her mind up and wanted nothing more to do with him. Why was he wasting time even thinking about her? There were plenty of other women, so why then was his devious mind making plans to see her again? To steer his thoughts off her, Daniel tried dating a couple of old girlfriends, but on each occasion the evening ended badly as they became aware of his lack of concentration and made excuses to leave early.

One of them, Carla, had tackled him bluntly about his motive for asking her out. "Before I leave, I would just like to know who I am being used as a stand in for?" she said sarcastically.

"Pardon?" he had blustered.

"I'm not entirely stupid, even if at times you treat me that way," she said, giving him an exasperated look. "I do know when the man that I'm with is either on another planet, or in love."

"Sorry, Carla," Daniel said, lamely.

"Seeing as it's you, I'll forgive your bad manners this one time." Carla tilted her head and gave him a twisted smile. She continued to stare at him, a look of satisfaction spreading over her face. "It makes a change to see the catcher, caught."

"What do you mean?" He gazed up at her as she stood up and retrieved her bag, his face wary.

Carla just gave him a knowing look, patted him gently on the cheek and left him sitting staring after her, his mind in a turmoil as he contemplated his own inexplicable emotions and behaviour. He slumped back in his chair with a sigh of irritation as he mentally crossed another girlfriend off his list. Was he that pathetically obvious?

"Come on, Zoe, it will be fun," Libby cajoled. "Just you and me and a nice fattening lunch."

She had called in at her sister's flat and was doing her level best to wrench Zoe away from her work for a while. Libby had discovered a little Italian restaurant not far from Tom's place and was trying to persuade her sister to join her.

"No hidden agenda?" Zoe eyed her suspiciously. "No unexpected surprises?"

"It's a simple lunch." Libby threw her hands up, her eyes wide, and shook her head. "Are you paranoid or something?"

"Both of the aforementioned," Zoe laughed, as the thought of food made her stomach give a warning growl. "Hang on, you've won me over. I'll just get my jacket; I am a bit peckish, as it happens."

When they reached the restaurant and smelled the food, Zoe was glad that she had accepted her sister's invitation. "Mm, it smells absolutely delicious." She looked across at the appetising food on their neighbour's plates, and felt her mouth begin to water. "Whatever that is, I'll have some."

They ordered and while they waited, Zoe glanced idly around, admiring the decor. The place had a cosy air and colourful pot plants placed strategically around the room made it seem friendly and inviting. Her wandering gaze halted, and she froze as her eyes focused on the two imposing men entering the door.

"You utter sneak," she hissed, glaring with narrowed eyes at her sister. "You promised no surprises, especially unpleasant ones. I ought to report you to the parents! Dad would soon deal with your treachery."

"A weak threat. I would soon get round him. A soft touch, as we both know," Libby scoffed.

"Okay, you won that argument," Zoe scowled. "Give me a reasonable explanation as to how Daniel has turned up here at exactly the same time."

"Coincidence?" Libby offered, staring back at her innocently.

"Don't give me that," Zoe scowled at her. "You can be so devious at times."

"Mind if we join you?" Jack's deep voice inquired as he made himself at home in the seat next to Libby and gave her a quick kiss.

"Yes," Zoe muttered pointedly, not deigning to look at the large man hovering over her.

"Of course we don't mind," Libby smiled. "Sit down, Daniel, and take no notice of my sister. She's in a grouchy mood today, I'm afraid."

Zoe flashed Libby a speaking glance and fixed her eyes determinedly on her plate. She would simply pretend that he wasn't there, although quite how she planned to do that when every pore in her body was conscious of his presence was something that she would have to work out as she went along. She heard the chair beside her grate as Daniel pulled it out and lowered himself into it, his arm brushing against hers in the process. She jerked away as if he had poured acid onto her skin, hearing his angry intake of breath at her instinctive reaction. So much for pretending that he wasn't there. His scent filled her senses, some cologne he used, and it appealed to that hidden side of her, coiling ready to strike. Zoe flushed and just hoped she could resist the urge to take a bite out of him. She averted her eyes and stared down at the table. It wouldn't do for him to catch that look, because she had a feeling Daniel wouldn't fight her off and would respond in kind. Besides, it would spoil everyone else's dinner. A faint smile curved her lips as Zoe imagined such a scene.

The conversation was stilted and only took place between Libby and Jack, who were very conscious of the two silent people sitting glowering on the opposite side of the table. It was almost a relief when a throaty voice interrupted the increasingly strained atmosphere.

"Darling, did you forget to ring me? Men can be so thoughtless." Janine gave a tinkling laugh. "You know I would have met you, darling, you only had to ask."

Daniel caught his cousin's eyes and narrowed his own, glaring at him as two arms slid familiarly down his shoulders. Jack shook his head imperceptibly, miming, not me.

"How does she do it?" Jack whispered, turning to Libby and frowning as he glanced at Janine. "She must have built-in radar where my cousin is concerned."

"Is there a chair here for me?" Janine looked helplessly around, fluttering her hands, smugly conscious of the stir her presence was causing in the restaurant, especially amongst the men. Of course, the brief clothing could have some bearing on it, or the fact that two well-known stars were dining together. Whatever the reason, it gained her the attention that she basked in.

"Please, take mine," Zoe stood up swiftly, simmering with anger. She'd had enough. "I have to get back to work now anyway."

Without so much as a thank you, the star pushed past her and slid into her vacant seat, carrying on as though Zoe had already gone, putting her hand on Daniel's arm and looking coyly up into his face.

Zoe was very tempted to pick up a plate of the succulent looking pasta and rub it onto the top of Janine's empty head. She would have been very surprised if she'd realised that Daniel's thoughts were running along parallel lines, except that he visualised pressing Janine's blonde head face down into a bowl of the juicy bolognese sauce and drowning her.

"Why are you leaving? Please don't go," Libby pleaded, catching up with her sister just as she reached the door. "I didn't know that awful woman was going to turn up."

"No, but you knew that equally awful man was," Zoe accused her. "I was so embarrassed and still hungry, I might add."

"Yes, well," Libby admitted, "perhaps that was a mistake, but you don't have to miss your lunch over it."

"Yes, I do," her sister said emphatically, "I am not sitting next to that...that... He makes me so mad I can't think straight. If you hadn't noticed, the table is meant for four. What was I supposed to do, sit on his lap when she arrived? I couldn't have eaten anyway with him there, so it's just as well Janine turned up, and anyway, what are you two doing even talking to him?"

"He was sorry," Libby said, shrugging her shoulders dismissively at Zoe's accusing face. "Daniel told us that the little discussion you had with him made him realise how wrong he had been to interfere."

"Discussion!" Zoe snorted, in disgust. "What discussion? All I did was make a complete and utter fool of myself. We didn't exactly talk, more like snarl. Well, he snarled, I screeched. Nothing went as I planned."

"Well, we've forgiven him. After all, he was only looking out for Jack. You can't blame Daniel for casting a wary eye over any females who get too close to his cousin."

"Huh!" Zoe sniffed disbelievingly as she stamped out, slamming the door behind her and imagining his head imprisoned in the gap, slowly being crushed. She stalked along the pavement, her feet grinding an imaginary backbone. Then her treacherous mind imagined his broad, bronzed body and her step faltered. My brain is going, she moaned. I've finally flipped, all I can think of is stroking him better. Zoe's stomach rumbled again, reminding her that she had missed a delicious lunch, all because of that man, and she began to torture him in her mind again, only this time she gave him no mercy.

Chapter Five

Any schemes Daniel had been working on appertaining to Zoe had to be put on hold when he received a frantic phone call from Jack.

"For pity's sakes, think of something, Daniel," his cousin pleaded. "Libby and I are trapped in my hotel and the place is swarming with press."

Libby and Jack's privacy had been too good to last. Up until now, apart from organised photo shoots, the young star had managed to evade the press, then someone had spotted him in a careless moment kissing Libby in public. The cry went up, 'Who is this woman?' Each newspaper wanted to be the first to identify his mysterious companion, and so the siege had begun.

Daniel was loathe to enlist the aid of Zoe, but he had no choice if the idea that had occurred to him was to be accomplished with any degree of success.

ᘯᘯᘯᘯᘯᘯᘯ

The last person Zoe had expected to see when she answered the ring at the door was Daniel. She was so bemused that she stood feebly aside as he barged in.

"Wear something sexy, instead of that sack," he said shortly, gazing down at her body encased in an old towelling robe. Damn it, she even looked mouth-watering in that.

"It's called a dressing gown," Zoe explained icily, then more angrily. "What are you going on about? Why should I wear something just to please you and why did I even let you in?" Zoe put her hand to her head, as though she couldn't quite believe her own stupidity.

"Sit down and be quiet," Daniel snapped, pressing one large finger firmly against her mouth as she opened it to protest. He gave her a penetrating look. "This isn't about us; it's about Jack and Libby. Ah! I see that I now have your undivided attention."

He removed his finger before it caught fire, he could still feel the heat from her soft lips, which seemed to be curling insidiously throughout his body. He took a calming breath and explained the whole awkward situation to her, stressing that he wouldn't have enlisted her aid, unless it had been vital to the plan.

Zoe only heard the last part of his conversation because she too, was trying to control the sudden irrational urge to press her lips back against his hand. It had felt so good, so strong, and she wanted so much to touch him that it made her breath catch in her throat. Then her attention was caught by his words and Zoe listened with a growing sense of panic, staring at him dazedly.

"We have to pretend to be them," Daniel said. "We must somehow throw the media off the scent until they've left the hotel and cleared the airport."

"Airport?"

"Yes, Jack's taking Libby over to France to escape while we act as decoy."

"You mean we have to act as though we're in love?" She gazed at him in growing horror as enlightenment dawned. "You and me... I can't."

"I know it will be hard," he snapped, visibly irritated by her obvious reluctance. "Try to think of it as a lucrative commission, which should appeal to you, shouldn't it? I will pay you very well for this night's work."

His head jerked back from the force of the slap that descended on his head, and he stepped back in shock. "What the hell is wrong with you?" he snarled, holding a hand to his ringing head.

"Don't be so damned insulting," Zoe raged. "You can keep your precious money; I know how terribly important it is to you. I will do this for Libby and then, thank goodness, I won't ever have to set eyes on *you* again."

"That suits me fine," he growled, still rubbing his cheek. They glared at each other, both hearts beating with anger and an unfathomable feeling of despair.

"I'll go and get changed," she said quietly, suddenly feeling deflated. She shut herself in her bedroom, leaving him staring at the closed door helplessly, wanting nothing more than to follow her in and push her down onto that nice soft bed.

Daniel strode up and down while he waited, telling himself that he was a pathetic fool. There were plenty of other women out there who would be only too happy to entertain him. She was nothing special, not even particularly pretty. He stopped as he realised that he was actually talking out loud.

Zoe's door opened and she came out, pulling her coat around her. "Did you say something?"

"No," he said dully. "No, just thinking aloud."

Daniel held the door open for her, and as she brushed by him, her perfume tantalised his nostrils, her soft body making him draw away sharply.

Zoe was aware of his instinctive movement and felt as though something had squeezed her heart. Surely he didn't find her that unappealing now, although after her previous antics, he probably thought that she would attack him if he so much as touched her.

In the rush to get to the hotel, Daniel only had time to add a few more details of his madcap scheme. It was enough to occupy her mind, and Zoe was able to put her own inexplicable feelings on hold.

"Remember, tough as it may be, just act the part." He gave her a tight-lipped smile. "We both have to be all over each other, and don't worry, it won't be for long."

ᘎᘎᘎᘎᘎᘎᘎ

The first thing they were aware of as they entered the lobby was the jostling crowd of journalists with the usual accompanying photographers. Zoe waited, hidden behind one of the large marble pillars that dominated the entrance hall, while Daniel skirted around the edge of the crowd, with his collar turned up and a wide scarf wrapped around his chin. He looked like some disreputable fugitive and Zoe suppressed a nervous giggle as she watched his furtive antics. He finally managed to push his way through the crush to the reception desk and huddled together with the red-faced manager, who was positively wringing his hands with anxiety. When he returned, she noticed that he was carrying a small bag as he hustled her towards the stairs and Zoe wondered what was in it.

"Why not the elevator?" she protested.

"Use your eyes," Daniel glanced around at her impatiently. "Does it look as though we can get near it? Besides, I don't want them to see which floor we're going to, they might just connect me with Jack."

Zoe stared at him; his words were not made from vanity. It was just a plain fact that with his height and build and the same dark good looks as his cousin, he needed to keep a low profile. Hence the hunched posture and lowered head. She smothered a laugh when he caught that look and frowned back at her irritably as they furtively ran up to the next floor.

The next problem was the group of photographers who were crowded in the corridor around Jack's door, being kept at bay by his bodyguards. It seemed that some determined members of the media had managed to slip around security, and the noise of chattering voices was deafening.

"Not to worry," Daniel said as he saw her concerned face. "Just stay close."

He bundled her into the room adjacent, so far without drawing attention to themselves. He shut and locked the door securely behind them, then crossed the room and opened a wallpaper covered door in the far wall. They found Jack agitatedly pacing up and down his room, with Libby lying on the sofa, her eyes red and swimming with tears.

"Oh! Thank God you came, Zoe. It has been awful. No matter what we did, wherever we went, they were always just one step behind us. We couldn't lose them, it was horrible." She sat up. "How did you get in here without them seeing you?"

"The manager let me have the use of the suite next door," Daniel held the key up. "It has an adjoining door."

"So, what is this cunning plan of yours?" Jack asked as he came to a standstill.

While Zoe commiserated with her sister, Daniel outlined his idea to his cousin, whose first impulse was to laugh hysterically, then he sobered. "That's so crazy that perhaps it might just work."

They all sniggered as Jack held his Tronicman costume up against Daniel's large frame. Jack himself was a tall, strapping six-footer, but his cousin was broader and heavier and topped him by three or four inches. The costume was going to be a very tight squeeze.

"Oh, God!" Daniel groaned as he came out of Jack's bedroom at last, "this is so damned humiliating."

The costume was stretched so tightly across his powerful chest and shoulders that it threatened to split and the zip at the back did not meet by several inches. The tights were positively indecent, even though for on-screen modesty they fastened at the back. Which was just as well, as they also did not quite pull up enough, and Daniel could feel the cool air on his buttocks. They hugged his strong muscular thighs lovingly, and Zoe found herself blushing as she gazed at the front where he was boldly outlined. When she glanced up again, she encountered his equally embarrassed face and put her hands up to her red cheeks. A slight smile tugged at her lips as humour gained the upper hand, and she started to giggle.

"What is so damn funny?" Daniel rasped, feeling as though he were encased in hot plastic.

"You are, we are." Her laughter increased. "You look so uncomfortable." She collapsed back into a chair, shaking with mirth.

He felt his rage increase; Daniel felt stupid enough without Zoe mocking him. He moved menacingly towards her and she shrank back stammering, "Now, look, don't you go all Neanderthal on me."

He felt as though the top of his head would lift as his rage escalated. "Neanderthal!" he roared.

"Now, now, children." His cousin stepped between them. "Remember us, the ones who are in trouble. Is this a private war, or can we all join in?"

Libby was observing them both with a speculative eye and smiled as she watched the two bristling people giving each other such hostile glares. The air between them was so brittle that she felt she could have shattered it with a light tap of her nail. Aha, so that's how it is, she smirked, this is more than just a passing attraction.

The two adversaries pulled themselves together and Zoe stood patiently as Libby eased a brown curly wig onto her head which she had taken from Daniel's mysterious bag, carefully tucking her sister's blonde hair out of sight.

"Hmm, not too bad, you could easily be mistaken for me if you keep your head lowered." Libby studied her carefully, pulling the wig further down over Zoe's forehead and pushing a few escaping blonde wisps firmly under the edge, while Jack threw the lightning blue cloak over Daniel's shoulders with a flourish.

"There, that will hide any gaps at the rear," he said, trying not to laugh at his cousin's discomfort.

"I can still feel the air on my backside, and how the hell am I supposed to walk in these damned silly boots?" Daniel moaned. "Look at this built-up heel."

"Stop whinging," Jack chuckled. "You get used to it. Think of poor old me, having to do it all the time."

"Yeah, but you get paid good money for looking like an idiot," Daniel grumbled. "I'll probably be hobbling within five minutes. I shall sue if they cripple me. Whatever possessed me to think that this was such a good idea?"

With his hair slicked back and the yellow eye mask in place, he bore a remarkable and striking likeness to Jack. Secretly both women thought that he looked magnificent, and Zoe had a job to keep her eyes away from those powerful taut thighs, which were so closely moulded by the hard stretched fabric.

"Right, onward all powerful Tronicman, and may the lightning gods lend you strength in your endeavours," Jack quipped with a broad grin.

His cousin cast him a dark fulminating look, gave a disgruntled snort and then looked down at Zoe. "Ready?"

She nodded, jumping as his arm snaked around her and drew her firmly against his side, her first reaction to pull away.

"Keep still," he said harshly, his grip tightening as his hand reached for the door handle, "and loving looks, remember, the show must go on. We have to present a believable image. Now clear off into the other suite, you two, and lock the door behind you."

Daniel pulled the door open, holding Zoe even closer. They were almost blinded by the multitude of flashes that immediately greeted them, and they bent their heads as the bodyguard's that Daniel had arranged for forced their way through the clamouring mob and closed ranks around the couple, fighting off the media as they escorted their charges into the elevator.

"Oh, my God," breathed Zoe, as she leaned weakly against the side. "Now I know what Libby meant."

"Yeah," Daniel said, "not a very pleasant experience, is it? I guess my cousin is used to this sort of thing, but not in his private life."

She felt even worse when she glanced across at one of the bodyguards and saw his gaze fixed admiringly on the shamefully low bodice of her dress, and she blushed furiously. Daniel's gaze sharpened as he saw the tell-tale colour surge into her face and his head swung around, his eyes narrowing coldly at the unfortunate man who immediately averted his wandering glance. Nobody in their right mind would want to take on this ferocious looking guy.

As they reached ground level, the door slid open, and they went through the whole draining performance again. Zoe heaved a sigh of relief as they scrambled into the back of a large, sleek black limousine, which was waiting with its engine running at the hotel entrance, ready to whisk them away.

"My eyes positively ache," she moaned as she blinked them, still seeing pinpoints of light long after they had driven off. "Are the press still following us?"

"I'm afraid so. We might have to drive around for some time before they realise that we aren't really going anywhere."

Daniel suddenly lunged for her and pressed her face into his neck. As her mouth opened to protest, she found her lips pressed against his skin just under his jaw and anything Zoe might have been going to say completely left her head. She could feel the hard contours of his body pressed against her side, and the hand that she had put on his chest to steady herself felt as though it had become welded to him. I wonder if I'm melting, she mused, as she leaned bonelessly onto him.

Daniel was also fighting an inward battle. If he moved her just a little, her soft body would rest more fully against him, and if he turned slightly, her mouth would be just below his. He felt an uncomfortable surge of desire. Oh, great! Just what he needed in this skintight costume. The chauffeur's voice interrupted his erotic thoughts.

"We've lost most of them, and the last car is pulling back, Mr Hammell, so you can relax."

Zoe tore herself away and sat up hastily at the sound of the man's voice. She felt incredibly stupid. For a few moments she had forgotten that Daniel was only play-acting and the disappointment she felt made her sigh with disgust at her own pathetic yearning.

After an hour of having been tirelessly pursued, all they wanted was to get back, get changed, and go home. They had given Jack and Libby ample time to clear the hotel, and they were surely on their way to the airport by now.

The two of them had hardly spoken, apart from the odd comments on the following journalists, and the atmosphere between them was filled with growing tension. Daniel didn't even trust himself to look at her, afraid that his eyes might give him away, and Zoe felt so miserable in the knowledge that she no longer appeared to hold any appeal for him that she sat in dark despair. She knew that she was being totally illogical, given the fact that Janine was on the scene, and yet couldn't stop this helpless longing that invaded her. She was caught up in a whirlpool of emotions, and all she could do was follow helplessly.

They arrived back at the hotel, tired and hungry, still being pursued by a few intrepid reporters on foot. The bodyguards escorted them up to their room and once inside, they slammed and locked the door with a sense of relief. Daniel went into the bedroom to remove his costume, and Zoe pulled the wig off her hot and itchy scalp, throwing the offending article down as she ran her fingers soothingly through her hair. She looked up as the bedroom door opened and her breath caught in her throat as she saw Daniel gazing at her with an odd expression. He was stripped to the waist, his broad muscular chest glistening with perspiration, and looked brooding and magnificent. He was also flushed and breathing hard.

"What's wrong?" she asked, her mesmerised gaze wandering freely over his tanned body. She blushed when she realised what she was doing.

"Damn stupid tights won't pull down," he said gruffly. "I need you to undo me. Jack put a couple of safety pins in at the back, and the bloody things are stuck."

"Oh, no! No, no, I can't... I can't." Zoe gulped.

She stared helplessly at him as he moved nearer, the thought of touching his naked back making her tremble. He didn't speak, and her eyes were drawn to the tight material that clung so snugly around his loins and was too revealing to hide his reaction as her gaze roved over him. Up this close, he presented a real danger. Colour flooded her face as she watched this evidence of his desire. Obviously, she had been in error as to his emotions, and heat surged through her, making her heart race.

"Damn," he groaned, as he tried to ease his discomfort. "For God's sake help me out of them. You will have to peel them off the top of my legs."

"I don't know if I dare," she whispered, a nervous smile on her face.

"Is there something you see that worries you?" he asked huskily, his discomfort momentarily forgotten.

"Frightens me," she replied. "I'm not sure how I should handle the problem."

"Oh, God," he said hoarsely, "don't say things like that, you have no idea what it conjures up in my mind."

Zoe laughed softly under her breath as she moved around behind him, unpinning the back of the tights, seeing the red weal on his buttocks from the large pins, and hearing the sigh of blissful relief as Daniel was released from his containment. She wasn't sure if that was a good or bad thing. Before she could move away, he turned and she gulped at the sheer overwhelming masculinity of the near naked man in front of her, only brief shorts preserving his modesty.

"Are you trying to tell me something?" she gasped, backing away from the advancing threat. Her voice died on a shriek as Daniel pulled her towards him and she was made very aware of how strong a threat it was. "Oh," she moaned, nearly fainting with the feelings he evoked as he pressed her more firmly against him. "We mustn't, we don't even like each other."

"Lust is good," Daniel whispered hotly against her mouth. As his body moulded itself more securely to hers, she felt her legs weaken and her mind ceased to function rationally.

Reality intruded on their private world before he could carry out any action they might regret, and it came in the form of a peremptory knock at the door.

"Oh, heavens," Zoe gasped as she frantically pushed free of his imprisoning arms. "Who can that be?" She looked down at the dress pooled around her feet, wondering how it had got there, glancing at her own near naked body, observing Daniel's aroused state, and embarrassment washed over her.

"Don't answer it," Daniel said softly as he reached for her again.

"No, please don't," she backed away. "It might be something to do with Libby and Jack." Zoe bent down and hastily slipped her dress back on as Daniel reluctantly turned back into the bedroom. "Who is it?" Zoe called, as she stood by the door.

She was shocked when a waspish voice announced from the adjoining suite, "It's me."

She whirled around to see Janine framed in the open doorway, and wondered just how much she had heard, or worse, seen.

"Just what is going on here?" the actress demanded as she stalked towards her with a suspicious frown.

Zoe stared at her, bereft of words, embarrassment at the situation making her swallow nervously, guilt at what she had nearly allowed to happen overcoming her.

"Nothing is going on," Daniel said, as he sauntered casually in wearing his trousers, and buttoning his shirt up. "We were just giving the press the run-around while Jack made good his escape."

He wondered how the hell Janine kept track of his movements. Perhaps she has got me bugged, he thought with frustration.

Daniel had not once glanced at Zoe since he'd entered the room, and she was again humiliated. It seemed that she had been used as a substitute once more, whilst he waited for his girlfriend to appear. Her lips thinned as anger coursed through her, masking the hurt. What was she, a spare part? Here she was still trembling, while he was acting as though nothing had happened and perhaps for him, nothing had. It was this thought that was destroying her. Well, she would never be used like that again, Daniel could look for another victim, she fumed, but inside she was crying.

"Sorry, darling. I mean, how silly can I be." Janine was mollified, as she cast a disparaging look at the dishevelled girl standing in front of her. "She's hardly your type, is she, darling?"

"Excuse me, I am still in the room," Zoe snapped, "and for your information, he isn't exactly my type either."

Daniel's head whipped around at this remark, and he regarded her with a dark enigmatic stare. "No, we're not at all suited, are we?"

"If you'll excuse me, I'll just get my bag, I want to go home," Zoe said, her small face frozen. "I assume we're safe to leave now."

"Quite safe," Daniel drawled, casting her an angry, perplexed look. He felt as though she had delivered a body blow. Why was she acting so oddly? Perhaps she was ashamed of her response, regretted it even, or maybe her mind had been on that wimp of a boyfriend? He couldn't think what Zoe could see in that weedy guy. Here he was offering himself on a plate and she couldn't care less. No words passed between them as he drove her home, partly because Janine monopolised the conversation, but mostly because they had nothing left to say to each other.

Zoe climbed wearily up the stairs to the flat and let herself in. It was cold inside, which only served to make her feel more miserable. She turned the heat up and made herself a warm drink, nursing it between strangely numb hands. Sitting hunched on the couch, she was distressed to feel tears welling up. She jumped to her feet impatiently, nearly spilling her coffee in the process.

"What did you expect," she sobbed, wiping the tears angrily away. "Did you really think that a man like him would look at you? Use you, yes, but love you, I don't think so." Zoe wept as she questioned her own poor judgement. "How can I feel like this when I'm not sure if I even like the man? Why did I mention love, and what's more, why am I talking to myself?"

Daniel was also busy berating himself for his own erratic behaviour. He wanted her, that was for sure, but anything deeper his mind shied away from. He really wasn't sure of his feelings, he just knew that she was embedded in his soul like the proverbial thorn, and she couldn't be plucked out. Women had always been part of his life. If they walked away, so be it, he felt nothing. If he left them, Daniel expected them to understand. Now he was left with a strange empty feeling inside at the thought of never seeing Zoe again, a new experience for him, and he was not a happy man.

Chapter Six

Since her last contact with Daniel, life seemed incredibly flat to Zoe. Her designs were progressing, but very slowly. She stared miserably down at her design pad, wishing that she had stayed in bed. She hadn't wanted, nor expected to fall in love, and to be so enamoured with such an unsuitable man was an error of judgement she would never have believed herself capable of. She gazed around at the various men in the design room. Why couldn't she have fallen for someone like them, nice ordinary men. Take Ted, for instance. A nice enough man, single...boring. She heaved a sigh. It was no good, she thought, they were halfway through the morning already and she simply couldn't concentrate on her work, making mistakes that would have been costly if one of her fellow workers hadn't rescued her.

Zoe watched him as he corrected her design measurements and frowned thoughtfully. She stared at Mike as he turned towards her. Now take him, for instance; there stood a perfect example of a normal man. He was charming, open, and understanding. She had even let him take her to meet his parents once, purely as a friend, no ulterior motive. He was a designer, like herself, and he perched himself casually on the edge of her desk as he dropped her work back, asking if everything was all right.

"Fine, thanks, Mike. Just tired, I guess." She glanced up at his friendly face. "And thanks for helping me out."

"No problem. It's not a man, is it?" he queried.

Zoe flushed, as she answered stiffly. "Why on earth should it be a man?"

"Ah!" he said meaningfully.

"What do you mean...Ah?" She stared at him crossly. Then her face relaxed into a rueful smile, as she saw the twinkle in his eyes. "Sorry. You're quite right, of course, it is a man. A very large and irritating one."

"Hmm," he murmured.

"You're doing it again," she laughed.

"So, what's the trouble?" Mike smiled sympathetically down at her. "Can I be of some help?"

"How?" Zoe asked.

"Well, if he's a problem, all is obviously not going well, and if you need to make him jealous," he grinned. "I'm your man."

Zoe gave him a disbelieving look. "Are you serious?"

"Don't worry, and don't be offended if I say that I won't complicate your life. Not that I don't find you attractive, but I'm suffering from unrequited love at the moment, and I am in the throes of pining," he sighed. Mike gave her a sad smile as he waited for her reaction.

"Somebody working here?" Zoe asked, glancing furtively around.

"No!" he laughed, "and if she was, you've just given the game away. Anyway, that is for me to know, and you to keep that out of." He touched the tip of her nose with a paint-smeared finger.

Zoe stared at his face while she rubbed at her nose with a tissue. Mike really was serious and wanted to help. Well, why not, she thought. After all, what are friends for?

"Actually, I don't want to try and make him jealous, it would be a complete waste of time. You have to be in love with someone to feel that emotion," Zoe sighed and propped her head on her hands. She looked up at him. "It's me that has the problem. Mind you, I would like the opportunity, just once, to show him that I don't care. Does that sound childish and silly to you?"

"Nope, I know the feeling," he said knowingly. Mike tapped his teeth with his pen, looking thoughtful. "Right, plan A, where does he eat lunch?"

"I wouldn't know, and anyway his office is up in town."

"Fancy a day in the city?" he raised his eyebrows inquiringly. "Let's play detective. We can lurk in doorways and wait until he leaves for lunch, then just shadow him. Even have our lunch in the same restaurant and spy on him."

"Okay, Sherlock, and what happens if the restaurant is exclusive, and you have to book?" Zoe folded her arms. "They would throw us out on our ear."

"Give me his name, and the address of his workplace," Mike demanded. He raised his brows as she passed him the required information. He had heard of the Hammell Group and wondered if Zoe knew just who she was dealing with here. Suddenly he jumped up and walked rapidly away, leaving her staring open mouthed after him.

She waited patiently for some minutes, but he didn't reappear. Shrugging resignedly, she picked her pen up and concentrated on her design again, wondering why he had vanished so quickly, unless he was having second thoughts about becoming involved. She was so immersed in her work that it made her jump when Mike materialised beside her desk with a distinct swagger, and tilted his head to one side.

"Who's a clever boy, then?"

"Let me guess." Zoe gave him a mock frown. "Okay, what cunning plan have you devised?"

"Simple, dear Watson, I phoned his office, spoke to the secretary, said I had a present to deliver." He paused to see if she was following his line of thought. At her wise nod, Mike carried on. "Told her I wouldn't be able to make it until lunchtime, and I would be most grateful if she could tell me which restaurant he dined in, so that I could leave the present there."

"Very clever," Zoe stared at him with open admiration. "And that leaves us where, exactly?"

"Patience," Mike smirked. "I then phoned the restaurant and asked if they had a spare table, and guess what?"

"Okay, shall I guess, or will you enlighten me?"

"They had a cancellation," he beamed. "Clever or what?"

"You're wasted here, you ought to work for MI6," she said mockingly, leaning back in her chair.

"I know, I know." Mike held his fingers up and studied his nails, with a smug expression. His plan was so simple that it might just work.

"Why are you going to so much trouble for me?" she asked, curiously.

"Fellow sufferer," he grimaced. "And it's for me, actually. I want somebody to see me going out with you, someone special."

It was Zoe's turn to say, "Ah!" and Mike laughed, as she giggled up at him.

Zoe wanted to know when plan A could be put into action. He informed her that there was no time like the present, and that he had booked a table for that very day. "What!" Zoe shrieked, looking down at her casual shirt and jeans in dismay. "Look at me, I've got to go home and change. I can hardly go dressed like this and what about our work, how can we square it with he who shall be obeyed?"

"Forward planning, you peasant." Mike glanced towards the office. "Us secret service types are always one step ahead. Remember the exhibition at Earls Court, tiles, and all that? Well, that's where we shall be heading after lunch. We can bring back samples from our competitors. Our overlord thought it was a great idea." He puffed his chest out, waiting for praise, a pleased smile on his face.

"You did well, Agent M," Zoe laughed. "Now, do I have time to go home and change?"

"Don't worry," Mike said, "I need a change of clothes, as well. How long do you need?"

"Give me an hour." She glanced at her watch, good job it was still early in the day. "I'll be ready, detective."

Zoe's heartbeat accelerated with apprehension as they approached the restaurant and walked in. She let Mike go ahead, waiting to one side while he established exactly where their table was situated, while she tried to peer through the crowded room to see if Daniel had arrived ahead of them. Having made sure that he'd not yet made an appearance, she felt more relaxed as the waiter guided them to a small table for two.

Zoe sat with her back to the door, grateful that the tables in her direct view were all occupied, so that when Daniel came in, he would be seated somewhere behind her. A group of businessmen came bustling through the door, making her turn her head, letting a curtain of hair screen her face, as she furtively glanced behind her. Her heart swelled with pain as she spotted Daniel. He looked tired and sank down at his table as though his surroundings held no interest for him. To her surprise, he was also seated at a table for two, and then her fragile hopes sank as she saw the tall, elegant woman who joined him. All Mike's planning had been a waste of time. Another one of his numerous women she supposed, despondently. Janine wouldn't be best pleased. She turned back to see Mike's interested eyes assessing the large man across the room. One look at Zoe's face had made it obvious who the target was.

"So that's the man in question." He studied the formidable looking Daniel with a slight feeling of trepidation. "Big, isn't he? I hope for my sake that you're right about him not being jealous."

"Would you be jealous, if you were sitting opposite a beautiful woman?" Zoe smiled wanly.

"I am," he said gallantly.

"You are a very nice man, Mike, and too good for this wicked world."

"I know," he grinned.

Zoe laughed across at him, feeling herself begin to relax again. At least Mike would get a free meal. She would pay, and he had earned it.

Across the room, Sylvia's eyes rounded as she saw Daniel stiffen in his seat. His eyes were riveted on someone behind her, his hand gripping his fork so tightly that his knuckles had turned white, and he had not heard a word of her conversation. She swivelled her head to see who had captured his attention. Nobody stood out, unless it was the slim, blonde-haired girl seated at one of the small side tables. Sylvia stared at her with a puzzled frown. What on earth did he see in her? Oh, she was certainly attractive, but nothing to compare with the glamorous women he usually escorted around town. Then the young woman lifted her face and smiled up at the waiter and became almost beautiful. Her eyes were huge, a clear shining blue, and when her mouth parted in a smile, her whole face lit up. Sylvia looked back at Daniel; he seemed to be totally mesmerised by this girl.

As if she became aware of his penetrating stare, the young woman turned her head, glancing back over her shoulder. She blushed as she encountered Daniel's narrowed eyes, and hastily averted her own, turning to her companion and engaging him in animated conversation. Sylvia stared in fascination at her cousin, and this time his gaze faltered as he became conscious of her close scrutiny.

"Sorry," Daniel mumbled, and cleared his throat with embarrassment. "Thought it was someone I knew." Then he picked up his knife and began to eat, studiously avoiding Sylvia's eyes. The rest of the meal was conducted in relative silence. She watched him shovelling the food in, obviously not tasting anything, and gave an amused laugh.

"My, my, you must be extremely hungry, I have never seen you devour food quite this fast before."

Daniel's head jerked up and he flushed as he caught the knowing look on her face. He threw his fork down in disgust. "Can't I hide anything from you?" he groaned.

"No, you can't." She put her hand over his and squeezed it. "You've tried to over the years, but it has never worked, has it?"

"You are like a ferret, trained to go in for the kill and you always were able to make me confess my secrets." He gave a reluctant laugh. Then he sighed, pressed his hand to his forehead and smiled miserably. "I give in. If you must know, I've got it bad, as you no doubt can tell."

"I guessed," Sylvia said softly as she returned his smile. She felt his hand clench under hers as the object of his desire passed close to their table on her way out. Her attentive companion was devoted to her, if his gently guiding arm and caressing hand were anything to go by. It was as though he couldn't wait to get her alone. Sylvia's eyes narrowed thoughtfully when she caught the gleam of amusement in the man's eyes as he flicked a quick glance down at Daniel. Something was off there.

ᘏᘏᘏᘏᘏᘏᘏ

Zoe had observed the clasped hands of the pair at the table, feeling despair at this evidence of his fickle nature, and Mike held her more closely as he felt her tremble. Her eyes were brimming with tears and by the time they had reached the entrance, she could no longer see where she was going. As a result, when they moved through the doors and stepped outside, her foot missed the top step and she would have fallen, had it not been for Mike's ready arms.

At that precise moment, Daniel was emerging from the entrance behind them. What he observed was Zoe being held tightly against the man's chest, laughing up at him, and it appeared to Daniel that she was clutching him back with equal fervour. He felt so enraged that Sylvia, just to one side of him, was shocked to hear a growl issuing from his throat.

Zoe looked up and gulped as she felt the impact of that furious stare, and pulled hurriedly away, rushing Mike off along the pavement. "Well, I think that worked, don't you?" she laughed feebly. "Daniel now thinks that we're an item."

"I thought you said that he wouldn't be jealous," Mike said, looking distinctly pale.

"Honestly," she protested, "I really didn't expect him to be. I think it's just that I'm the one who got away, and he doesn't like it."

"He doesn't own a gun, does he?" Mike threw his hands up. "What am I talking about, why would he need a gun when he could just tear me to pieces with his bare hands."

Zoe couldn't help it, she creased up, and then they were both laughing helplessly as they ran, although her own laughter verged dangerously close to tears. When they had sobered up, she linked her arm through his, and sighed despondently. "Seriously though, thank you for trying to help, but I really don't feel like going to that exhibition now. All I want to do is go home."

"Come on, it'll help take your mind off the hulk for a while," he said. "We have to go; the boss won't be too pleased if we turn up empty-handed."

Zoe gave in and they spent two hours trailing around the show stands, selecting samples, and Mike was right, it did help to occupy her thoughts.

Sylvia stared curiously at Daniel as he drove her home, she had never been hustled out of a dining room that quickly in her life. "If this girl lives as far away as you say she does, don't you find it rather odd that she chose to eat in your favourite restaurant today?"

"Perhaps her boyfriend likes eating there," he snarled.

"Daniel, for heaven's sake look where you're going," she cried out in faint alarm as he looked away from the road, swerving as he glared across at her.

"Then stop talking of something you know nothing about."

"Oh, dear, do I detect an awesome degree of jealousy?" Sylvia drawled.

"Do you want me to crash this bloody car, woman?" he muttered.

Perhaps it would be wiser to change the subject, Sylvia mused, as she glanced at his flushed face. "How is Jack doing, has he managed to keep the press away from Libby?"

She had heard everything about Jack's involvement with his young lady, but nobody had thought to mention this latest development with Daniel. Sylvia felt a mixture of pity and exasperation as she glanced across at her cousin. He loved this girl, even if he, himself was unaware of that fact, and the lady in question had such a wounded look in her eyes that it was pretty obvious she returned his feelings, so what was keeping them apart? Perhaps she ought to get herself an invite and meet Libby, find out a bit more.

ᘎᘎᘎᘎᘎᘎᘎ

Zoe was slumped in the seat next to Mike on the train, staring vacantly off into space. He glanced at her sympathetically.

"The way it turned out wasn't one of my better ideas, was it? Perhaps I should have minded my own business."

"No, please don't blame yourself, Mike, I didn't have to take you up on it," she said listlessly, laying a consoling hand on his arm. "At least I know where I come in the grand scheme of things, absolutely nowhere. I was completely wasting my time."

She just wished the other women in his life knew that they were wasting their time, as well. It seemed to her that Daniel was not capable of sustaining a serious relationship. She couldn't understand why she was so deeply attracted to him and began to wonder if there was something in her makeup which was drawn to unreliable men. She was silent for the rest of the journey and when Mike left her at her door, it was with a feeling of deep concern. He decided that it would be his duty to keep an eye on her. She was vulnerable at this stage, and that big surly guy looked the type to take advantage of the fact.

When Zoe let herself into the flat, her sister took one look at her face and rushed to her side, putting her arm around her shoulders. "What's wrong?"

"Nothing," she replied as her face crumpled, and she started to cry.

"I can see that," Libby said sarcastically. "You always howl when you're happy."

Zoe sniffed as she tried to speak, blotting her face with the tissues that Libby had thrust into her hands. "I'm in love with a great big, horrible, obnoxious, hulking brute and I think I must be losing my mind."

"Who are we talking about?" Libby enquired, trying to suppress a smile, having a fairly good idea of who the man in question was.

"Nobody," Zoe mumbled. "Just someone unattainable. I am so stupid, I could have chosen someone normal, but no, not me, I have to want somebody who is a total chauvinist pig."

Zoe turned to the bathroom, throwing her coat onto the chair, then she stopped in the doorway. "I'm going to have a shower. I won't use the bath," she announced dramatically. "No need to worry about me drowning myself."

Libby did feel worried. Her sister looked so miserable. She had seen that Daniel was attracted to Zoe, yet like her sister, thought that Janine was more than just a friend to him. Libby sincerely hoped that he was not trifling with Zoe, because he would answer to her if he was. Her sister didn't give her heart lightly, and to the best of her knowledge, had never felt this deeply before

about a man.

Chapter Seven

Life dragged on for Zoe, her sister had at last gone home, leaving her in peace, and she still visited her brother's place once a week. She felt that it was now safe to do so, as Jack had gone back to America to film his latest adventure, which meant that she shouldn't have the misfortune to bump into Daniel again. Tom had tried his best to get her interested in one of his friends and he was a nice enough man, but she had no desire to meet him on more intimate terms. Besides, Daniel seemed to have taken up residence in her brain, and she had no chance of forming a relationship with anyone else, until she had learnt to erase him.

Zoe scoured the sink viciously, imagining it to be his body, her teeth gritted as she visualised him begging for mercy. The trouble was that her mind twisted the image, making her hands begin to caress his hard muscles. She growled and went at the task with more vigour, casting out images of bronzed flesh.

"Wow!" Her brother's voice interrupted her torture plans. "He must be really smarting."

"Pardon?" Zoe looked up startled, she hadn't heard him come in.

"Whoever it is on the end of those vengeful thoughts, and my sink was surely not that bad."

"Oh, don't be an idiot." She flung the cloth into the sink and rinsed all the skin and gore away, or was it only water?

Zoe laughed when she turned around and saw the way Tom was backing warily away from her, his hands held up as though warding her off.

"I am perfectly sane now," she assured him. "I've worked it all out of my system."

"Are you sure about that." He eyed her doubtfully. "Or are you looking for someone else to vent your spleen on."

"Will you back off!" Zoe narrowed her eyes and gave him a fearsome frown. "If you want to pacify me and stop me from attacking you, make me some coffee, I deserve it after the good job I made of your sink."

"If that's what it takes to calm you down, I will make some gladly," Tom grinned. "Coffee is the antidote, is it?"

"To what?" she queried.

"To soothe the savage beast," he laughed. "The one attacking my kitchen."

"You're pretty good, for an irritating young brother," she giggled.

Tom always had a calming effect on her. He could make her smile and feel good about herself again, and she loved him for it. She remembered back to all the crushes and broken relationships that her brother had steered her through. Her lips twitched as she thought of them, they had meant nothing. None of them had developed into anything meaningful, and yet she had still acted as though it was the end of her world. Libby had always been there for her, of course, but Tom was the one who could lift her spirits and make her see that life still had plenty to offer. Zoe studied him as she sipped her coffee, listening to him talk about the day's filming. It was a wonder no one had snapped him up as yet, he would make a wonderful husband for some fortunate woman.

Zoe found herself scanning the newspapers for pictures of Jack, and of course, when she did come across them, there was Daniel in the background of some, with Janine clinging like a limpet to his arm. There were even some coy hints about the relationship, which made her heart ache as she read them. It seemed odd to her that sometimes the articles seemed to concentrate more on Daniel rather than the fact that he was Jack's cousin, and this gave her pause for thought. He must be a well-known name on the social scene, given his wealthy business contacts and the glamorous actress always at his side.

She sat gazing into space with the latest speculative offering as to his romantic intentions crumpled between her hands. I must like pain, she sighed. What did he see in that woman? Apart from the fact that she was totally beautiful, a well-known star, had a figure to die for, and was obviously available to him whenever he wished. Beat that list of attributes.

She stood up and threw the paper into the recycling bin, then wandered over to the mirror studying her face and figure closely. She wasn't too plain. In fact, I'm quite attractive, Zoe thought. Maybe I should cut my hair? She pondered on that, turning her head, first one way and then another, holding her long blonde hair up with one hand, and pouting her lips, and then laughed sadly; she couldn't walk around with such obvious intent. Anyway, no matter what she did, it would still be her. Hardly any competition for the other girl. No, let's face it, she told her reflection, this is you, take it or leave it. Find someone more suitable to shower your affections on. The only problem was that her mind wouldn't follow her dictates, and continued to throw his image up, making her despair at her own lack of willpower.

As the weeks went by, Zoe found herself thinking more and more about Daniel, not less. Not seeing him was eating at her. She couldn't cast him out, and tried to occupy her mind by throwing herself into an endless round of parties with friends. She began to visit places of interest, museums, gardens, theatres, but always he was there, like a huge dark spectre at the back of her mind.

The summer promised a heatwave and Zoe lay face down on a rug in Libby's small back garden. "This is the life," she sighed, and stretched luxuriously, feeling the soft warmth seeping into her skin and bones, making her feel languid and at peace with the world. "It's so blissful and mindless, I could stay here all day."

Libby was leaning back on a lounger nearby, reading a magazine and taking the occasional sip at a cool drink. "If you did," she announced in an admonishing tone, "you would just shrivel up like a prune in this hot sun. You should have put a hat on."

"Don't lecture me," Zoe pleaded, without opening her eyes. "I haven't got the energy to retaliate. Don't be such a nag."

"You know that I'm right," her sister said, glancing down at her with a frown. "Look at your back, it's turning pink already."

Zoe summoned her strength up and struggled into an upright position, sitting cross legged, while she tugged her old muslin blouse on to shield her shoulders and then crammed an old straw hat of Libby's onto her hot head. "Satisfied?"

"I am now," said Libby sternly, then spoilt it by breaking into a giggle as she observed her sister's comical appearance. "You look like a scarecrow."

"Thank you, evil sister," Zoe said, her lips curving into a broad smile. "You boost my morale no end."

Libby laughed back, pleased to see Zoe acting a bit more like her old self. The ring at the door made them both jump, and Zoe looked at her sister in consternation, hoping that if it was Jack, he would be alone.

"Is Jack due back yet?" she asked Libby with a worried expression.

"He usually always rings before a visit," she answered with a slight frown. "It may just be Tom."

She was right, it was Tom, but he wasn't alone; Jack and Daniel entered just behind him.

"Surprise," Jack said, gathering Libby up into his arms and giving her a resounding kiss. "I managed to get away a couple of days early." He whisked her away into the house for some privacy and Zoe was left alone with Daniel, her brother already having made a beeline for the kitchen in his eternal quest for food.

Zoe wished that she was anywhere but there. Apart from the fact that she looked like something the neighbour's dog had dug up, she felt totally unable to cope with Daniel, yet face him she must. She sat looking at him from under the brim of the floppy hat, her eyes in shadow, drinking him in. He looked so virile and handsome sitting precariously on one of Libby's small patio chairs, his bulk dwarfing it. Her heart had begun its usual pounding rhythm that the sight of him always caused, and she wondered if he could hear it. She was so busy studying him, her eyes glazed, that it was only when she blinked that she found herself sinking into the blazing green depths of his equally intent gaze. She blushed and turned her head away, taking a sudden interest in the flowers that bloomed so profusely around the borders. She didn't want him to gain the impression that he held any attraction for her whatsoever.

A large shadow fell over her. It was certainly not a cloud, and she felt herself grow even hotter, so she kept her gaze fixed on the small arch that leaned drunkenly in the bottom corner of the garden, hardly able to withstand the weight of the roses that festooned it.

Daniel sank down beside her. "Are you going to talk to me?"

She didn't answer, lying face down again, hoping that if she kept her eyes tightly shut, he would go away and leave her alone.

"I know that you're not asleep," an irritated voice said as the silence lengthened.

"Fat chance," she sniffed, "with your voice grating on me, keeping me awake."

"You can't just ignore me, you know," Daniel said, his voice edged with frustration.

"Who can't," Zoe said rudely, her manners deserting her as she panicked, which only served to make her blush even more. "Sorry, that was inexcusable."

"Yes, it was, but I forgive you," he said curtly, his nostrils flaring angrily. "Although I don't know why I should."

"It's immaterial to me whether you do or not," she snapped back, burying her face into her arms, as though to block him out.

Her skin prickled as she heard him change his position, and she was aware of him shifting nearer to her. Curiosity made her turn her head and open her eyes, only to wish that she hadn't as she found herself staring straight into his half-closed eyes. He was sitting much too close, regarding her with a determined expression, and she wriggled uncomfortably.

"Feeling nervous?" he asked, silkily.

"No." She cleared her throat. "No, why? Should I be?"

She turned over onto her back, which was a mistake, she realised, as he immediately leaned over her, moving so swiftly that she was given no chance to evade him, and his arms were placed firmly either side of her body, restricting her movements.

"What are you doing?" Even to her ears, the breathy voice that issued from her throat sounded feeble.

"Making sure that I've got you in a position where you'll stay long enough to listen to what I have to say," Daniel growled. "If only for a few minutes."

The problem with his good intentions was that they easily evaporated at the close proximity of her delectable skimpily-clad body, and against his own better judgement, he found himself lowering his head, his eyes fixed on her softly parted lips.

"Oh, no, you don't." Zoe took him by surprise, as with a violent push and sinuous ease, she scrambled clear of his imprisoning body and jumped up, making her own head spin at the sudden movement. "I don't think what you had in mind was talking," she said scathingly, unable to prevent herself from shaking. "I call that taking advantage of me when I was helpless."

"Helpless!" Daniel gave a snort of disbelieving laughter, then stood up and walked purposefully towards her. "We still have to talk."

"I don't think we have anything of much importance to talk about."

"Damn it! Why won't you listen to me?" he said, through clenched teeth. "You never give me the chance to explain."

"Well, it really doesn't matter, does it?" she said wearily. "We hardly see each other and as it happens, I simply don't have the time. I really must go home and get on with some work."

"So, since I arrived, you've suddenly remembered a mountain of work you have to get through," he said grimly. "At least I have some effect on you."

"Don't flatter yourself," she snapped, feeling desperate to get away. She couldn't handle this verbal sparring with him. "You have no effect on me at all."

"Is that right?" Daniel's face suffused with anger. "Well, you won't mind if I kiss you goodbye then, will you?"

His hand shot out and held her face in a firm grip while his lips descended equally as rapidly and took her mouth captive, the force of his kiss rendering her temporarily mindless. He drew back, staring down at her confused face and a bitter smile twisted his lips.

"Tell me that did nothing for you," he said, his eyes daring her to tell him that she hadn't reciprocated.

"It did nothing for me," Zoe whispered in a faint voice as she pulled away from his restraining hand and put what she hoped was a safe distance between them. She heard Daniel's grunt of annoyed disbelief as she scurried into the house to inform Libby that she was leaving. Tom escorted her home, trying to jolly her out of the dark cloud that enveloped her.

"Sorry, Tom," she gave him a sad smile. "I'm not very good company today, am I?"

"Don't you feel well?" he asked her, not knowing the true cause of her misery. He knew, of course, that she found Daniel attractive, but didn't realise just how deeply the man affected her.

"Just a nagging headache," Zoe replied, smiling at this understatement. It was her heart that was aching, a pain that she was slowly becoming used to.

ᘎᘎᘎᘎᘎᘎᘎ

Zoe had some holiday due and decided to go and visit her parents. Her mother was always asking her to go and stay, so she arranged to spend a week with them. It was what she needed, a total break. Her parents had now settled on the outskirts of a small Sussex town, within a short walk to the sea. It was a quiet place, the beach near them being a long way from the main seaside resort and that tranquillity appealed to her at this moment. At the last minute, with her parents' consent, Zoe invited Mike. He had sounded so down when he had last called that she had felt sorry for him. He was good company, and he was so uncomplicated. Also, he had taken her to visit with his parents when she had needed to escape her problems. Now it would be nice to return the compliment. He had eagerly jumped at the chance to take some time off, and they had duly made the arrangements. So, here they were, walking slowly down a country lane in the hot sun, towards the sea.

"It's so peaceful here." Mike breathed in deeply, filling his lungs with the fume-free air, and threw his arms wide, embracing the view. "This is pretty spectacular. You could forget all your troubles here, couldn't you?"

"Yes, I sometimes wonder why I don't make the effort to visit more often," she agreed. "When I get back, I always feel as if I've had a good rest, at peace with myself, you know."

They veered off along a narrow track which led them towards a small inlet, following the shore around through the tall pines that lined the crumbling edge of grass and mud, until it blended with the stones and small pools of trapped water the sea had left behind. It would soon return. Shallow ripples were already lapping back towards the small creatures who inhabited them and were waiting patiently for fresh food. A ceaseless circle of life in their tiny world. Mike found it all fascinating and couldn't wait to explore the pools. He felt like a kid again.

The narrow stretch of water began to open out into a larger area, where boats were pulled up onto a pebble beach. As they strolled further along, there were high banks of grass and stones, that ran down in gentle slopes leaving all traces of vegetation behind as it became a finer shingle and merged with a wide band of warm, golden sand running down to the sea.

The gulls and the sea were the only things disturbing the silence as the waves sucked at the beach with soft greedy sounds, and the only other person in sight was a lone fisherman, a small speck in the distance standing patiently by his line. Beyond the banks of shingle were small, isolated cottages and fishermen's huts, their shuttered and empty windows lending a strangely desolate air to the scene. Choosing a suitable spot, they flung their towels down, peeled off their outer clothing and headed for the sea. Plunging in, they frolicked like children, shedding their inhibitions and laughing uproariously over their own silly antics. For a few glorious moments there were no cares or pressure to intrude on their time.

After over an hour in the water, Zoe indicated to Mike that she'd had enough, and made for the beach. She towelled herself dry, looking along the shoreline at the fisherman still waiting with infinite patience for a bite. I suppose it's nice and peaceful fishing, she thought. Not her thing, of course, yet just watching him made her feel tranquil and she envied him his peace of mind.

Mike stayed in, swimming leisurely along the shoreline, whilst Zoe sat wrapped in her towel, eyes closed, her face lifted to the sun, glorying in this sense of freedom. Invariably her thoughts turned to Daniel. What was it about this one man in particular that drew her so strongly? She felt as though she had been invaded by a force stronger than herself, one she was not equipped to handle. The feelings that had taken possession of her soul frightened her. Was love always this painful and debilitating, she wondered, and why did she have to fall for someone who couldn't return those feelings? Zoe berated herself, trying to turn her thoughts away from him.

She opened her eyes, shading them with her hand as she gazed around, trying to spot Mike. He was still out there, floating on his back, thoroughly enjoying himself. She smiled at his pleasure, turning her eyes to the horizon. To sit and look out into that endless vista always had the same calming effect upon her. She felt small, a tiny piece of the jigsaw that made up the stuff of life, and it had always put her troubles into perspective, until now.

As she stared at the distant line between earth and sky, a face floated into view, an unwelcome face. She was tempted to raise her hand and swat at it. "Please go away," she pleaded. "Leave me alone, let me forget you."

She didn't realise that she had breathed the last words aloud, until Mike's voice said plaintively, "How can you forget me; I'm right in front of you."

"Sorry, Mike." She flushed, and then laughed at his comical expression. "Just gnashing my teeth out loud."

"Doesn't work, does it?" he stated, sinking down beside her, vigorously towelling himself dry.

"You too?" she asked, giving him a sympathetic look.

"Yep, same here." Mike drew his mouth down. "Don't get me wrong, this has been great, a complete change."

"I know," she replied. "I also know that it's not so easy to forget, try as we may."

She glanced sideways at Mike. He was a nice-looking, presentable guy, with a charming personality. Why couldn't she have set her sights on him? He was so much less complicated than Daniel whose presence disturbed her so much. Mike simply made her smile, but had never tugged at her heart strings. They gathered their belongings together and wandered back in silence, not appreciating the sounds of the birds singing, the bees humming busily as they collected nectar from the wildflowers that grew in the hedgerows, or the call of cattle and sheep, both too deeply immersed in their own unhappy thoughts.

When the time came to go home, Zoe felt quite sad. Her mother came into the bedroom while she was packing and watched her fold the clothes into her suitcase, neatly and methodically.

"I'm glad that I taught you to do something right," her mother smiled, then her mouth firmed, as she studied her daughter's unhappy face. "Who is it?"

"Pardon?" Zoe's head came up and caught her mother's gimlet eye fixed upon her.

"As nice as Mike is," her mother observed, "it's not him, is it?"

"No." Zoe sank down beside her case. "It's not him. In fact, it's someone I would be better off not knowing."

"He's not a criminal, is he?"

"Only if you think that breaking hearts is a crime. Not that he's even aware that he has," Zoe sniffed. She gave a watery smile. "And since when have you known me to consort with criminals?"

"Oh, darling, I'm sorry." Her mother smiled, then looked at her with concern. Her arms closed around her daughter, as she sank down beside her. "Are you sure about his feelings?"

"Certain," Zoe said, wiping ineffectively at her welling eyes, grateful for the handkerchief her mother proffered.

"You know that you can come and stay anytime," her mother assured her. "When you feel that it's all becoming too much."

"You'll be seeing an awful lot of me then." Zoe gave her a wobbly smile.

Her mother returned her smile and gave her a comforting hug, then changed the subject, not wanting to upset her further. Quizzing her on Libby's latest conquest and asking if this time it was really serious.

"I think so, mum," Zoe said, drying her eyes and pulling herself together. "She was talking of bringing him to see you and dad soon, so you'll be able to judge for yourself."

Their mother couldn't get over the fact that her youngest daughter was dating a famous star. In their world it was almost bizarre, and her parents, like Zoe, were concerned that Libby could be badly hurt if it all went wrong, which they suspected it eventually would. Zoe did her best to reassure them about Jack's intentions.

"Wait until you've met him." She gave her mother a rueful smile. "I was quick to judge too, although I think that, like me, you'll soon be won over. I don't know if it will last, but at the moment they seem to get a great deal of pleasure out of each other's company."

ꟷꟷꟷ

Mike glanced across at the silent girl beside him in the car. "Are you okay?" he asked quietly. "I won't give you a penny for your thoughts, I guess I know them already."

"Shows that much, does it?" Zoe gave him a faint smile as she leaned her head back on the seat. "Pathetic, aren't I?"

"If you are," he answered with a wry smile, "then so am I."

Zoe glanced at Mike, her curiosity making her question him on his own rocky love life. "What exactly is happening in regard to this special woman of yours?" she asked.

"Nothing," Mike replied, despondently. "That's the trouble. She's just got over a rather tense relationship, and I'm not sure if she actually even sees me when I speak to her. I can't seem to make any headway at all."

"Oh, Mike, I am sorry," Zoe said, frowning in sympathy. "Are you sure she isn't just taking things slowly, you know, sort of feeling her way with you?"

"Perhaps you're right," Mike stared at her, digesting her words, adding thoughtfully. "Maybe she's wondering just how serious I really am. I'll just have to try bit harder, won't I? Make myself indispensable."

She returned his smile. From little things that he'd previously mentioned, she had a feeling that this mysterious girl was more attracted to him than Mike realised.

Chapter Eight

Zoe was concentrating on her designs when the doorbell rang. It was probably Libby come to enthuse about Jack again, and she wasn't sure that she was in the right mood to listen. She carefully put her work away, stood up, and stretched, sighing impatiently as the bell pealed again. As she made her way down the spiral staircase, she glanced at the hall clock and frowned. It was a little late for Libby. Then her frown cleared as she remembered that her sister had been to visit with their parents, which must be why she was calling at such an odd hour.

The smile froze on her face as she opened the door and looked up, and up again, into Daniel's mesmerising green eyes. "No," he said, stepping forward and catching the door as she pushed at it. "Don't shut the door in my face."

"We have nothing to say to each other," Zoe said, her voice a whisper, feeling threatened and overwhelmed by his presence.

Daniel pushed past her and stood trying to gauge her mood. She was still standing by the door, her whole body radiating with a tension, which left him in no doubt he was not welcome.

"We have plenty to say," he said curtly. "Stop pushing me away."

"I thought from your previous behaviour," Zoe said venomously, "that it was precisely what you wanted. Let me refresh your memory. Did you, or did you not, try and split Libby and Jack up?"

"They've forgiven me. Why can't you?" He stared at her defeatedly.

"I'm sure that you don't need me to console you," she said coldly. "Where is Janine, by the way?"

"Let me explain about her," he pleaded, moving towards her.

"It's late and I'm tired," Zoe snapped, backing away nervously. "I'm sure the explanation will be a long and colourful one, and I don't particularly want to hear it, so please go, and let me get to bed."

Daniel stared at her, his imagination working overtime at the thought of Zoe in her bed. She blushed as she caught the look in his eyes, and a wave of heat washed through her.

"Look." He hesitated. "Obviously, I've caught you at the wrong time. My fault. The need to see you overruled my common sense. It's late, you're tired. If I leave now, will you promise to meet me tomorrow?"

"I don't want to meet you, tomorrow or any other day, thank you."

"I won't leave until you promise," he threatened.

She could tell by the determined look on his face that he wouldn't budge until he'd extracted such a promise from her. "Oh, very well," she said reluctantly, feeling her resolve softening at the relieved look in his eyes. She found herself, much to her own vexation, weakly agreeing to meet him at his office in town and then go on to lunch.

Zoe shut the door behind him, leaning against it with a sense of relief, listening to the sound of his footsteps receding as he ran down the stairs. To her own ears, her palpitating heart sounded like a drum, and she wondered that he had not heard the thunderous sound.

ᘈᘈᘈᘈᘈᘈᘈ

When the next day dawned, Zoe bitterly regretted her decision. It meant leaving her open to more pain, yet there was no way she would go back on her word. Her mother had always taught her that a promise should always be kept, and the lesson was deeply engraved. On her way up town, she sat thinking deeply about Daniel. He'd assured her that there was a perfectly reasonable explanation for Janine's constant presence, yet the part of her that lacked confidence nibbled at the fact that he was such a virile man. She didn't doubt that he was very attracted to her, but would that attraction last? Should she, as Tom decreed, take a chance on love, even if that love was only on her part? She didn't even know why she was wasting time questioning herself. She loved him so much that she was helplessly swept forward. She had no choice but to travel this road.

A short time later she hesitated outside his office, staring at his name boldly outlined in gold lettering on the door, then glanced nervously along the imposing plushly carpeted corridors, suddenly feeling overwhelmed by the sheer overpowering size of the place, and wanted to turn tail and run. Why she had even agreed to this made her question her own sanity. She remembered all too well her last encounter with his secretary and flushed, wondering how she would be greeted, then she squared her shoulders and pushed the door open, only to stop in shock at the scene that confronted her.

Time seemed to stand still, and she felt as though she were moving through treacle. The secretary stood with her back to Zoe, looking towards the two people outlined in the inner doorway. Daniel was locked in a passionate embrace with Janine, and didn't see Zoe standing as though turned to stone observing him, but the actress did and gave her a small, satisfied smile.

Zoe had heard the term broken-hearted used before, but had never experienced, until now, the awful shattering truth of those words. She blindly put her hand out seeking support, feeling that she would fall if she released her vicelike grip on the door frame. Her other hand pressed tightly to her mouth to stem the wail of pain that was clamouring for release. She had fallen straight into this humiliating situation, and it was all down to her. How could she have trusted his word?

Snapping out of her horrified trance, she moved her stiff body, stumbling from the scene as though she were dying.

Her slight movement caught Daniel's eye, and he turned his head looking towards the door, but there was no one there except his secretary Margaret hovering anxiously, her face flushed with exasperation. Daniel unclasped Janine's arms and pushed her away angrily.

"I don't wish to appear rude, but as you no doubt can see, I am an extremely busy man," he indicated the paperwork and computer on his desk and the two men waiting patiently on the chairs beside it, watching the proceedings with great interest. "Now will you please refrain from visiting my place of work."

Darling, Daniel, I am so sorry," Janine pouted and gave him a quick kiss, stroking his cheek and giving him a flirtatious look as she turned away. "You are such an old cross patch sometimes. I'll see you later. You may be in a better mood then."

He sighed with frustration as she sashayed out of his office, and he gave his secretary a wry smile. "I know that she's extremely exasperating to deal with, Margaret, but could you please think of some excuse, short of murder, to stop her the next time she shows her face?"

Margaret tutted in vexation, then laughed in commiseration as he scrubbed at his lips with tissues taken from her desk. Most men would be delighted to have a beautiful film star pursuing them. It was a pity that Janine's nature didn't match her good looks. The silly vacuous face that she showed to men was completely at odds with the one that she presented to women, and Margaret found her distinctly unpleasant.

"I shall do my very best, Mr Hammell," she assured her boss, determined not to let that dreadful woman slip past her again.

Daniel glanced down with concern at his watch and marched back into his office. "I'd better get a move on if I'm to meet Zoe in time for lunch."

Zoe felt frozen, her emotions held tightly within her as she made her way home on the train. She ignored the attempts at conversation the only other occupant of the carriage made and the young woman, sensing a deep conflict going on in the distraught girl opposite her, made no further overtures.

Not until Zoe had gained the sanctuary of her home did she give way. She sank down onto her old comfortable couch, curled herself into a ball, and great tearing sobs tore through her body as she lowered her defences, letting her humiliation and grief overwhelm her. Daniel had just clearly proved to her that she had been right about him in the first place. If she hadn't turned up just that little bit early, she would have been none the wiser and probably would have swallowed his carefully rehearsed lies without question. So, Janine meant nothing to him, did she? Well, from where she had been standing, that wasn't the impression she had gained.

She lay quietly staring dully up at the ceiling, her emotions now cried out. She'd learned a valuable lesson today, not to trust him, a mistake that wouldn't occur again. To be fair, Daniel had made no commitment to her. All this heartache was purely one-sided. She stirred herself and sat up, wiping her damp swollen eyes, wishing that she could shut her feelings off. The sudden ringing of the phone, the sound shrieking through her body, made her tense and gasp. She stared at it warily, not wanting to answer, not daring to in her fragile state, sensing that it would be Daniel wondering where she was, and in that moment, she almost hated him.

She stood up slowly, feeling devoid of energy, and wandered out into her kitchen, automatically reaching out to switch the kettle on for coffee. It was force of habit rather than the desire for a drink, and at this moment she needed the comfort of its warmth, inside and out. Glancing up at the clock on her wall, she was surprised to note that an hour of her life had passed whilst she had been immersed in her misery, and that fact frightened her. She sank down at the kitchen table, head in hands, gazing down into the swirling liquid in her mug. Her eyes were aching. In fact, she was aching all over, as though she was sickening for something. Was this the effect that unrequited love had on one, made you feel brittle and ready to fall apart?

She lowered her hands and gripped the mug, feeling the soothing warmth beneath her palms. The sudden intrusive sound of the phone ringing again made her tremble, spilling some of the hot coffee over her fingers, the pain destroying her defences once more. Her eyes blurred as the tears welled up, spilling over, running unchecked down her face, and dripping steadily from her chin. She couldn't move; she simply didn't have the energy to answer that demanding ring. She couldn't bear to listen to *his* voice offering yet more silly excuses.

Daniel, still grasping the phone in frustration, was at his wits end. Zoe had promised to meet him and then had simply not turned up. Now she wouldn't answer her phone, and he had been trying to contact her for the last two hours. He could have explained to her about Janine, if only she would hear him out. What had he done wrong? Could he have been mistaken in thinking that she was attracted to him? Daniel had an unpleasantly hollow churning inside at the thought of Zoe not returning his feelings in any way. He picked up the phone for one last attempt. There was no reply.

ꟷꟷꟷ

Zoe sat staring at the sketch pad in front of her, trying to make sense of the squiggles that adorned the page in front of her. Her creativity seemed to have deserted her, and she knew exactly who had caused this loss of concentration. She rubbed her hot eyes tiredly. If she was completely honest, she knew that she was just as much to blame. What she needed was a complete change in her life. Staying with her parents, even with Mike as an amusing companion, hadn't worked its usual magic and the complication of Daniel had still confronted her when she returned. Something more drastic was called for, so she began gathering brochures from local travel agents, determined to get away somewhere warm and interesting, where she could completely forget about that man.

"Why don't you try Canada?" was Libby's idiotic suggestion. "Don't look at me as though I've suddenly gone mad. I know what you're thinking."

"Oh, do you, and what does this look of disbelief convey to you?" Zoe asked sarcastically.

"That you have a Daniel fixation," her sister replied, adding hastily. "Now, before you explode, listen."

Zoe made her way to a comfortable chair and then with exaggerated movements sat down, folding her arms, regarding her sister with solemn eyes, her head tilted in a listening position. "I'm waiting with bated breath for you to enlighten me. Do carry on," she said primly.

"Daniel is a very large man, as we all know," Libby began, frowning as her sister gave an exaggerated sigh, at this seemingly useless nugget of information. "Yet, as strange as it may seem, he isn't spread all over Canada. To my knowledge, it's a very big country and there are actually some places where he cannot find you."

"How can you be so sure?" Zoe challenged her.

"Because," Libby said slowly, as though talking to a child, "we will not tell him where you've gone."

"Ah! That might work," her sister smiled, then grimaced at Libby's unimpressed face. "Okay, so I'm paranoid where he's concerned, but it is his home country."

"Are you sure that you don't want him to find you?" Libby narrowed her eyes at Zoe's flushed face.

"Of course I'm sure," Zoe said sharply. "What a stupid thing to say. He knows where I live, he can find me anytime he wishes to."

"Hasn't called lately, has he?" her sister observed.

"No, why should he?" Zoe muttered defensively. "The number of women that he's got on the boil probably keeps him too busy and I'm glad."

"Really? Now, let's see," Libby drawled, holding her hand up and ticking her fingers off one by one, as she spoke. "So, Canada is large, Daniel cannot leave the country because he is swamped by a sea of women, and you, as a result of the aforementioned point, will be perfectly safe. An ideal situation."

"Oh, for heaven's sake," Zoe huffed. "Stop trying to psychoanalyse me. Yes, I am desperately in love with him, and just as desperate to escape him. I need to know that I can get away somewhere that I won't be disturbed, and no, I won't be able to forget him in a hurry, but I will have a darned good try."

"Sorry," Libby gave her a small apologetic smile. "I know I do go on a bit, but I want you to be happy."

"I will be happy if I can get away from people who keep reminding me about Daniel!" Zoe stated in exasperation.

"I would like you to meet a big, dark, handsome man, who will turn out to be just what you're looking for. Someone like Jack." Libby sighed as she gazed at her sister. She paused. "It sounds as though I'm describing Daniel, doesn't it?"

"Honestly, there's no use talking to you, is there?" Zoe said crossly. "You can be such a pain at times. Give it a rest, will you?"

"All right." Libby held her hands up. "All right, I will back away from the subject, I promise."

Zoe stared at her suspiciously. Her younger sister didn't give up on a problem that easily. She was planning something.

"Don't you interfere," she warned her, pointing her finger like a missile. "I won't forgive you if you do."

"Duly noted, sister dear," Libby said blithely as she gathered her coat and purse up in preparation to leave. "I'll keep my nose out, I promise."

"I'll hold you to that," Zoe called out as her sister disappeared down the stairs.

"Have you ever known me to break a promise," was Libby's parting shot, her laughter echoing loudly up the stairwell as she left the building.

"Yes," Zoe sighed, as she shut the door. Canada was out, that was a certainty.

ꟷꟷꟷ

Wales was her final destination, not quite what she had in mind, but the sun was hot at this time of year and the skies had obligingly stayed clear for the last two weeks. The forecast was for more of the same and Zoe was looking forward to the welcome break. At least it was getting away by herself. Time to sort her mind out along with her priorities.

Mike had been talking at work about the idyllic holidays he had spent in Wales as a child and had still enjoyed well into his teens. It was only his work and various girlfriends which had interrupted these annual vacations. Now, although he went abroad more often, he still remembered with great fondness his enjoyment of the small village near the sea where he had once stayed.

Zoe had sat at her desk, her face cupped in her hands as she listened to him reminisce. She had felt a faint stirring of interest. The place had sounded remote and peaceful, and the thought of sea and sand, with mountains thrown in for good measure, held a strong appeal. "Where is this paradise?" she had questioned eagerly. "You make it sound so tempting."

The next day Mike had given her the address of the cottage that his parents had stayed in, describing how it sat in the fold of a hill, overlooking the bay.

"It sounds gorgeous," Zoe said wistfully. "Do they still rent it out?"

"As far as I know," Mike replied. "Mum stayed there the year before last, so I imagine it is still available."

Zoe had made her plans, making sure that she fitted in with her colleagues' holidays and then she was off.

ᒥᒧᒥᒧᒥᒧᒥᒧ

Now here she was on the train, watching the scenery unfold as she travelled to her much-needed bolthole. Her breath drew in as she caught a glimpse of mountains in the far distance. She could feel her whole body responding to the sense of freedom that filled her at the sight and relaxed into her seat, sighing contentedly. The sun was shining with a vengeance, and by the time she had stood outside the tiny station waiting for a taxi, Zoe was positively wilting. Her clothes were sticky, uncomfortable, and crumpled. She was drooping with fatigue when she finally reached her destination and stepped from the cab, and was therefore extremely grateful when a smiling grey-haired woman as wide as she was tall, with no seams in between, welcomed her in and presented her with a much-appreciated cup of tea.

"This is so kind of you, I feel a bit jaded after the journey." Zoe sighed with pleasure, sipping slowly at the refreshing liquid.

"You'll soon cool down in here. These old stone walls keep the heat out and you may find yourself having to use extra blankets. It gets quite cold and damp in here at night no matter the weather," the woman said as she gave Zoe a warm smile. "I'm Mrs Hughes, by the way. Call me Meg, my dear, everybody else does."

She bustled about, gathering up a basket and her coat. As Meg went to leave, she paused in the doorway and put the key to the solid old front door onto the table. "I'll leave this with you, cariad, and I shan't bother you again, but if there's anything at all that you need to know, just call in. I live just down the lane, first cottage you come to, you can't miss it. There's also a little shop further on down the lane, you'll find that it stocks most basic essentials. Oh, and the bus comes by once a week if you need to go into town, or there's the bread van. Emlyn will give you a lift in an emergency. Now enjoy your holiday."

"Oh, that's good to know. When does he call round this way?"

"Once a week," the other woman beamed.

"Helpful," Zoe murmured, in faint disbelief. Let's just hope any emergency only occurred on the one day he happened by.

Meg was right, the nights were cold and damp, but the comfortable old bed and cosy duvet kept Zoe warm and snug. She slept deeply and dreamlessly that night, something that she hadn't done for quite some while. She was woken in the early hours of the morning by the soft sound of rain falling steadily onto the roof and she smiled sleepily as she lay listening to the gentle drops pattering against the windowpane. Her smile faded as it became heavier, the pattering developing into a sound more like small stones being hurled at the glass, and then the heavens opened, and summer was gone.

"Good grief," Zoe whispered to herself as she sat up and observed the water now cascading down her windows. The next thing she became aware of was that she was freezing. "My first full day and winter descends. So much for my beautiful view of the mountains."

The rain was relentless, and the wind had become a continual thunderous roar that buffeted the old cottage and kept her sealed in as effectively as if someone had locked her away. Any attempt to step outside nearly tore the clothes from her body. This continued on and off for a full week and between downpours, mist still obscured any view that she may have had of the sea, or anywhere else for that matter.

On the evening of the last day, when the rain still showed no signs of abating, she felt moved to shake her fist at the sky. It was only mid evening and yet it could have been night, the sky was so dark and overcast.

"Why me?" she moaned. "Why wait until I go on my holiday to have the worst storm of the century? Have I even jinxed the weather now?" As if in answer, a streak of lightning lit the sky and the violent crack that followed made her jump nervously. "That's it, I've had enough," Zoe stated firmly, shaking with reaction. "I'm going home tonight."

When the knock came at the door, she assumed that it would be Meg, come to check up on her, the kindly Welsh woman having called once or twice before to see if all was well.

Zoe rushed to open it, her words of greeting dying on her lips as she let out a piercing shriek. She nearly collapsed with shock at the huge apparition that appeared outlined against the sky, illuminated by another brilliant flash of lightning.

"Take it easy," a deep familiar voice soothed her. Zoe peered more closely at the large drooping figure, her nerves still pulsating with fright. Libby had broken her promise. She would definitely kill her.

"Oh, God, I'm being punished," she muttered as she squeezed her eyes shut in disbelief. "The devil has sent the manic demon of lightning to destroy me."

"Let me in," he said forcefully. "It's hell out here."

"Well, you should be familiar with that," she sniped, unable to resist the crack.

"Very funny." Daniel gave a false laugh. "Now, are you going to let me in, or do I have to pick you up and move you? Your choice."

Zoe backed away immediately. She had no wish to feel his hands on her. Now, that was a blatant lie, yes, she did. It made her heart palpitate just to think about it, but that was not how she was supposed to feel, she was here to forget this Casanova.

"What are you doing here?" Zoe glared at him defensively, as she reluctantly allowed him to enter.

"I had business up this way, and Libby was worried about you."

"That's a flimsy excuse," she said, disbelievingly. "Since when has my sister worried about me when I'm on holiday."

"You obviously haven't heard the news." Daniel stared down at her puzzled face. Apparently, her family had been very concerned when reports of the appallingly bad weather had reached them. The television news coverage had numerous recordings of terrible flooding, and they'd had visions of Zoe being marooned, maybe in distress. When they heard that Daniel had some business to transact in a neighbouring county, they had asked him to detour and check up on her for them. "So, you see, they had good reason to worry," he told her.

"Yes, well, I'm sorry," she said grudgingly. "It was good of you to take the time to call."

He gave her a resigned look. "We both know why I'm really here, don't we?"

"No, I don't," she assured him, her heart thumping painfully.

"Yes, you do," he snapped.

"No, I do *not*," she emphasised.

"You damn well do," Daniel roared, moving towards her.

"What is this," Zoe shouted at him, submerging her fear with anger, "a pantomime?"

"It might just as well be," he snarled. "You have been virtually hissing at me from the minute I arrived here."

"What did you expect, I came here to get away from you..." Her voice rose in panic as she tried to rephrase that telltale sentence. "I mean people."

"So, you are worried about having me anywhere near you," Daniel said with quiet satisfaction. She didn't like the way he was smiling smugly at her, or the look in his eyes. If Daniel thought that because she was trapped in this isolated cottage with him, he could have his way with her, he was sadly mistaken. This spinster was going to fight her dastardly suitor off.

She didn't deign to answer, and turned her back on him as she finished the packing that she'd started earlier. Part of her wanted to fuss over Daniel and make him remove his wet clothes, they were actually starting to steam. The sensible side knew that it was safer to let him suffer; he was far less dangerous that way.

"What are you doing?" he stared at her in disbelief. "You can't leave at this time of night."

"Oh, yes, I can," Zoe stated obstinately.

"Let's not start all that again," he sighed. "Let's face it, it would be the height of stupidity to go out in this weather. We'll have to stay here tonight."

"I am *not* spending the night with you," Zoe said sharply.

"Who asked you?" he growled. "If you keep your hands off me, there will be no problem, will there?"

"You...you," her voice failed as anger overwhelmed her. Zoe turned around, grabbed her case, and marched into the bedroom, slamming the door shut. She let her case fall, put her hands over her face and shuddered, taking deep calming breaths. A few more minutes of that and she would have flown at him and heaven knows what the consequences of that action would have been. Humour welled up as she visualised herself trying to attack Daniel's large solid form, and she gave a slightly hysterical giggle.

She sat down on the edge of the bed, totally unable to relax, yet not daring to go back into the small living room. For all she knew he may have divested himself of his wet clothes and the very idea of being confronted by him in that state was an unnerving thought, also a very erotic one. She chastised herself for her vivid imagination and getting up, she walked to the door, locking it quietly, then jumped as his voice sounded just behind it.

"I'll make myself a cup of coffee then, shall I, being as I'm cold and wet through?" Daniel's sarcastic words floated through the panels, irritating her, yet they also had the required effect of making her feel guilty. She could almost feel him listening on the other side of the door, waiting for her to reply. "You can't be asleep already," he bellowed, annoyed by her lack of response.

"If I had been, I wouldn't be now, would I?" she shouted back. "Did you call me just to tell me that you've learnt how to make coffee? How on earth did you manage to find the time between women?"

"What women?" Daniel yelled in frustration.

Zoe refused to answer and watched as the handle twisted. The thump that followed made her back away, but he didn't follow it up.

Daniel sank down onto the old, battered sofa, his arms spread out along the back, shaking his head. So much for getting her alone and clarifying the situation. If he was bald when she next saw him, it would be her fault. She made him feel like tearing his hair out. Zoe seemed to have a fixation about him and other women. He couldn't think where she had gained that impression from. He smiled wryly, perhaps he should be flattered by her assessment of his prowess. He sighed. All he wanted to do was talk to her. No, if he must be honest, that wasn't all he wanted, but he could wait until she learned to like him a little more. He wondered just how long that would take. At his present rate of progress, a very long time. At least while he was here with this weather trapping her in, he might get the chance to really discuss things with her. Not that he had much time left; she would be leaving in the morning. Although not until lunchtime. He brightened up, plenty of opportunity to straighten things out.

Zoe heard him banging cupboard doors, the sound of a spoon in a cup and then silence. She listened carefully, her ear pressed against the door, but no sound followed, and she could only conclude that he must have fallen asleep on the sofa. She undressed and huddled down in her bed, but sleep eluded her, and she moved about restlessly. The poor man had made a detour just to see if she was all right. Okay, Daniel had more than that in mind, but he had certainly suffered for it. He had been dripping wet, and she hadn't even offered him a warm drink to comfort him. She wasn't usually so rude. It went against the grain to treat any visitor like that, even him, but there was no way that she was venturing out of this room tonight. It would be courting danger, given the way that Daniel had been pursuing her up until this present time. After their last little encounter, she was surprised at his present restraint. He hadn't once tried to touch her. Not that I want him to, she assured herself.

Zoe turned over, gazing at the window, watching the rain run down the panes and listening to the drum of the torrential downpour as it cascaded over the roof. She found it strangely comforting as she snuggled down in the safety of her bed, and wrapping the duvet securely around herself, fell asleep, lulled by the constant hypnotic rhythm.

Early in the morning, she woke and lay blinking, noting with wry appreciation that the sun was streaming through the windows. Well, it would be, wouldn't it, she grumbled to herself, I'm going home today. She jerked upright, shocked out of her warm cocoon under the duvet as she remembered who was in the living room. She leapt out of bed and dressed hurriedly, then opened the door slowly and peered out furtively. She let her breath out. Daniel was sound asleep on the sofa, and she pressed her fingers to her mouth at the sight of his semi-naked body only partially covered by an old blanket.

Zoe found herself unwillingly fascinated by his male beauty, the perfection of his solidly muscled torso and strong arms holding her mesmerised, unable to look away. It would be so easy to capitulate and get involved with this gorgeous specimen of manhood, but it was against her nature to have a casual and short-lived affair. She simply wasn't capable of handling it. Besides, there was the ever-present Janine. She shook her head sadly, closing her eyes briefly before she turned away.

She glanced around the room at his clothes. They were scattered over various items of furniture to dry, but the place was too cold and damp to do much good. Zoe put her hand out and felt his thin shirt, that at least was nearly aired. She glanced at him with concern as she realised that he was shivering, and walked hesitantly towards him.

Zoe bent down and reached out to wake him, her hand hovering nervously over the tanned flesh of his broad shoulder, but she feared to touch him. It wasn't his reaction that worried her, as much as her own. It brought a smile to her lips, and a blush to her cheeks, as she envisioned herself making advances to this virile man. He might have liked it, but it was never going to happen, not of she wanted to keep her dignity along with her sanity.

She straightened up abruptly, moving rapidly away from him and went out into the small kitchen, making as much noise as possible, deliberately banging the cupboard doors, stirring vigorously at the tea, hoping that this would be enough to wake him up, but he still didn't stir.

Zoe sat down opposite the couch, putting his tea on the small table between them and nursing her own cup between her hands, then sat staring at him, drinking him in. He must be utterly exhausted after his journey to sleep so deeply. She leaned forward studying him, looking at his strong, handsome face with longing. Then she frowned, did he look slightly flushed, maybe even feverish? As her eyes devoured him, he moved and stretched, and she got up hastily, nearly spilling her tea as the blanket began to slip, then gave a gasp of relief as she saw that he had at least kept his underwear on. She rushed to the window, displaying a sudden intense interest in the view, such as it was through the swirling mist, as his eyes began to open.

Daniel's pained groan made her turn, nearly dropping her cup. He was sitting hunched forward with his head in his hands.

"What's the matter?" she asked with growing concern.

"My head is pounding, my throat is sore, and I feel like death." Daniel gave a slight cough. He spared a glance at her. "That should please you."

"Don't be so silly," Zoe reprimanded him. "I sometimes wish that I could boil you in oil, but I wouldn't want your death on my conscience."

"And you don't think that boiling in oil would have the same adverse effect?" His sarcasm was spoilt as he sneezed violently. He grimaced, pressing his temples. "Oh, God, I think I really am dying."

"It's a cold," she scolded. "Not the bubonic plague."

She handed him his tea, instructing him to drink it down while she found some pain relief for him. Zoe gave him some tablets and watched as he swallowed them carefully, his throat obviously paining him. A slight smile pulled at her lips; some men were such babies. When they fell ill, they seemed to regress into childhood. Experience with her father and Tom had taught her that nobody suffered like men; they complained loudly and at length. As if to prove her point, Daniel began to grumble. Nothing was right, the tea was lukewarm, the sofa was lumpy, he hadn't slept, he ached all over, even his hair ached, and his clothes were still damp.

She listened patiently to his litany of woes, then conceded that he had a point, his clothes were still damp and creased. So, reluctantly, she went in search of an iron, to see what she could do with them.

She tried her best, but had to hide a smile when Daniel stood in front of her in his still slightly crumpled suit. Her amusement fled as he swayed weakly, and she rushed to his side, supporting him with her arm as she led him back to the sofa. Well, at least she hadn't been presented with the problem of fighting him off. In his present state, he simply wasn't capable of it. As if trying to prove her wrong, his other arm closed around Zoe, and he pulled her against him. She struggled and pushed him away.

"What do you think you're playing at?"

"I need comforting," he said softly. "Don't you feel sorry for me?"

"I did." She wrenched herself away and stood up, smoothing her dress down and glaring at him. "Save your clutching hands for all those other deluded females."

"I haven't got the strength to argue." Daniel lay back tiredly and closed his eyes. "I really did just want the comfort of you beside me."

Zoe stared at him, wanting to believe his softly spoken words, not trusting him, and yet found herself weakly sinking down beside him. He gave a sigh of contentment as he leaned his head on top of hers, his arms holding her close. His breathing deepened, and she realised that he had drifted off to sleep almost immediately. She lay limply against him, loving him, wanting him, allowing her hand to rest on his broad chest, and fought the urge to let her fingers explore the tanned skin showing through his unbuttoned shirt. The heat of his large body resting so intimately against hers was also causing something of a problem. It would be so easy to give in to her own desires, press her lips to that inviting mouth and wake him. In the mood Daniel was in, he wouldn't have resisted taking advantage of the tempting offer. She closed her eyes and sighed, knowing it would be a foolish mistake, and could only rebound on her. A few moments of gratification for him and crossing that line would only bring lasting unhappiness for her.

Zoe waited until his hold had slackened and then extricated herself carefully from his arms. It wouldn't hurt to let him rest whilst she cleared up ready for the off. She frowned as she studied his flushed face. So much for lustful thoughts. He really did look under the weather, and she began to feel genuinely worried about him.

Daniel awoke feeling weak and disorientated and watched through half-closed eyes as Zoe moved quietly about. He wanted to explain how he felt about her, but felt so ill that he really couldn't think of the right words to say. Besides, making advances whilst sneezing all over her in an old damp cottage was not quite what he'd visualised as a romantic setting. At this present moment, the only place that he wanted to be was in his own bed at home, so that he could die in peace.

Zoe looked up as she heard him mumble something about bed and shook him gently. "We can't stay here," she said sympathetically. "I've phoned for a taxi, and I've booked us into a hotel for the night. I think you need to see a doctor. You certainly can't travel far in this condition." She didn't know if he'd understood her words or not, his eyes looked glazed and hot, and they closed before she had finished speaking.

The taxi-driver was a thin wiry man, his frame belying his strength as he made easy work of taking most of Daniel's weight and helped Zoe walk him to the cab. They could both feel the heat emanating from the large man stumbling between them, and the driver expressed his concern about him travelling in such a state.

"We couldn't stay here any longer," Zoe explained. "Our tenancy finished today."

The driver was the sort of man who could draw your life history from you, and she found herself explaining how Daniel had come to be in this condition, and that a doctor would be seeing him as soon as they reached the hotel. They really did pay the odd visit in remote communities such as this. They didn't have to, and it wasn't expected of them. It helped that the doctor was old school, and he had spent his life ministering to the locals. Also, his practice was on the same street and only two doors away. Then she basked in the driver's approval as he nodded in agreement on her plans, and helped guide Daniel into the hotel.

Zoe felt unable to relax until the doctor's visit was over and Daniel was safely tucked up in bed, having been given something to alleviate his sufferings and make him sleep. Up to this point, she hadn't left his side. Now she explored the comfort of the other bed. It looked far too inviting to ignore and she threw herself down on top of it, spreading her arms out blissfully, totally relaxed. At least she didn't have the problem of explaining why she'd only taken one room. The simple fact was that they'd had only this one room available at the time of booking. She was extremely grateful on entering the room to find twin beds facing her. That was one problem dealt with. She gradually became aware of a gnawing hunger and stood up wearily, stretching, trying to iron out her aching muscles. Daniel was a heavy man and even with the taxi driver's help, she knew to her cost she had supported that weight. After checking quietly to see if Daniel was still asleep, she left the room and went in search of nourishment.

ᘎᘎᘎᘎᘎᘎᘎ

When she returned half an hour later, she put her head cautiously around the door. Daniel was still sleeping, but he was stirring restlessly. She crept forward and pulled at the tangle of sheets, which were trapped uncomfortably around his body. Zoe straightened them, trying to ignore the amount of firm muscled flesh she was leaning over, and felt his forehead. He was still very hot to the touch, but not quite so bad, which came as a relief. She pulled up a chair next to his bed and sat gazing at him, her heart in her eyes, moved by the sight of this large man made vulnerable by his illness. She must have drifted off, the food having lulled her into a somnolent state, because she had not been aware of him leaving the bed until a crash made her jump, bringing her instantly awake. Daniel was leaning drunkenly against the door of the small bathroom, his face pale, drawing in deep breaths.

"Why didn't you wake me?" Zoe cried, scrambling up and going to him. "I would have helped you."

"There are some things that I don't need your help for," he said in a slurred voice. "I managed perfectly well."

"It looks like it," she tutted, her arm going around his waist as he veered precariously close to a small table holding a floral display. "At least let me help you back to bed."

Daniel leaned gratefully on her, trying his best not to let too much of his weight bear down on her, but the effort of his trip to the bathroom had drained his strength, and he collapsed weakly back as she guided him onto the bed. His mumbled thank you faded into a whisper as he immediately sank back into a deep slumber.

Zoe went to move away but was halted by the hand that had closed around her wrist. She looked down at his closed eyes suspiciously. Was he feigning sleep? She peered closer and he sighed, turning over, his hand drawing her with him, so that she lost her balance and fell forward onto the bed. Now what? she thought vexedly, pulling at his imprisoning fingers, yet didn't want to wake him, but his grip had tightened, as though even in his dreams he had sensed her attempt to escape, and she knew that to break away would disturb him. He badly needed to sleep, so she sighed in resignation and arranged herself as comfortably as she could beside him. She lay rigidly, listening until his laboured breathing became quieter, her skin tingling with awareness at his close proximity, grateful that at least she was on top of the covers and not pressed closely against that virile semi-clad body. Gradually sleep claimed her, and unaware, she relaxed and snuggled against the large warm shape next to her.

The lips that were caressing her face felt wonderful, so warm and inviting. She smiled as she woke. That was some vivid dream! Her eyes shot open, rounding as her vision was filled by Daniel's face hovering directly above hers, his eyes gleaming with appreciation at the soft body pressed closely against him.

"What are you doing?" Zoe screeched in panic as she struggled up, frantically pushing him away.

"Kissing you," he explained patiently.

"I know that," she snapped, trying to keep her voice steady. "Get off me."

"It's my bed," Daniel pointed out. "You're the one who climbed in with me."

"You ungrateful beast," Zoe hissed through gritted teeth. "It was for your benefit."

"Exactly, and I was showing you my gratitude." He gave her a slow sensual smile, pulling her back against him, lowering his head and capturing her lips once more. Moving his mouth gently, invitingly over hers.

"No," Zoe protested, wrenching herself away from him and scrambling off the bed, her heart palpitating. A few more minutes of that and she would have weakened, becoming another notch in his belt.

"No?"

"Well," she huffed sarcastically, trying to gain control of her erratic breathing. "I can see that you're definitely feeling much better."

Daniel leaned up on one elbow, watching as she ran her fingers through her long tangled hair, and he said softly, "I wouldn't have taken it any further, you know, not without your consent."

"So, kissing me while I was asleep was not taking advantage of me?" She cast him a sceptical look.

"You seemed to be enjoying it," he drawled smugly.

"You unmitigated lower specimen of pond life," she said hotly, irritated as she recalled her waking response to his touch. Adding nastily, "I thought it was someone else."

"I see," he said slowly, his voice edged with anger. "Did I match up?"

"No!" Zoe said baldly, picking up her case and throwing things in haphazardly.

"Is that it," he frowned. "Just, no?"

Zoe ignored his query, straightened her crumpled clothing, and opened the door, pausing as she turned and looked back at him. "I have no wish to discuss which slot I'm supposed to fit into with your list of women." She gave him a withering look. "Goodbye."

"There are no women," Daniel sighed despairingly, staring grimly at the door as it slammed behind her. He lay watching the door long after she'd gone, wallowing in his misery. What was it about this particular woman who tugged at his heart strings in such a soul-destroying way. The sensible thing to do would be to forget her, yet Daniel's devious mind was already planning ahead on a way to see her again.

Chapter Nine

The first thing Zoe did after she had settled in at home was to go out again, and her destination this time was Libby's house. She was going to give her sister a piece of her mind, although she could ill afford to spare it, she thought, with a self-derisive smile.

She stood on her sister's doorstep, waiting for an answer, having just hammered determinedly on the door. Zoe saw the curtains twitch, then Libby's voice sounded just behind the door. "I'm not in."

"Open this door and let me in right this minute," Zoe demanded, "or your death will be even more prolonged and painful than I'd already planned."

The door swung open, and Libby backed away as an irate Zoe marched in. Before Zoe could speak, Libby held her hands up, palms out. "I know, I know," she pleaded when she saw her sister's accusing look. "I broke my promise, but you must admit that there were mitigating circumstances."

"Okay, I grant you that," Zoe said. "Now you tell me why you couldn't just have telephoned me?"

"Um...the lines might have been down," Libby improvised.

"Won't wash," her sister said flatly. "You have heard of a mobile phone, I take it."

"Did you take yours with you?" Libby tried to look surprised.

"Sometimes I could smack you," Zoe gritted. "You can imagine my shock when Daniel turned up, and before you start pumping me for salacious gossip, nothing happened. We just ended up having a slanging match." She flushed slightly as she remembered their tussle and hoped that her sister didn't notice the telltale colour flooding her cheeks.

"Oh, well," Libby said in an attempt to pacify. "At least it made a break for you. The view alone must have been worth it, with all those beautiful mountains to gaze on."

"Mountains, what mountains? I should have been so lucky," Zoe said shortly. "Even when the rain stopped, the mist obscured any sight of them. I feel as though I've been on a magical mystery tour. The difference being that I knew where I was going and I knew where I was when I got there, I just couldn't see it."

"So, the holiday turned out to be anything but," Libby said, laughing at her sister's woebegone face. "Perhaps Canada wasn't such a bad idea."

"Maybe you were right, after all," Zoe gave a reluctant laugh. "Although next time I go on holiday, you'll be the last person I tell."

For the fourth time, Zoe screwed up a piece of paper with an unworkable design on it. She felt like tearing her hair out. Would she never be able to erase that darn man from her brain? When the phone rang, she automatically put her hand out to pick it up, nearly dropping it again as Daniel's disembodied voice made her jump.

"Please don't hang up," he said quickly. "All I ask is that you meet me. Choose where you like but give me one more chance to talk to you."

Zoe stared at the phone, her hand gripping it tightly, wanting to slam it down, but somehow she found herself weakly agreeing once again to meet with him. Her chosen venue was the Italian restaurant. It was small and very public. There was no way that he could make any unwelcome advances in full view of the other diners, so she would feel as though they were on safe neutral ground. Tomorrow she would listen.

She had every intention of keeping their appointment, until she unfolded the newspaper the next morning and glanced casually through it. There on the front page was a large picture of Daniel leaving his office building, with Janine laughing up at him, under the heading, 'Star and latest conquest.' Daniel had his hand up towards the camera, as though to block the lens, as though not wanting to be seen. Well, that certainly put her in the picture, literally. There was nothing like having it spelled out for you. He was playing some devious game with Zoe as his novelty of the moment. Well, she would no longer help him play it, not anymore. She'd been acting the fool for long enough. Her face set with pain and bitter determination. She wouldn't be keeping their date, that was a certainty, he'd hurt her for the last time.

Daniel sat staring stonily at the door of the restaurant. He'd been there for over an hour with no sign of Zoe, and was finally admitting to himself that she wasn't going to show. He rose, seething with frustration and anger. This was the second time she had stood him up and he fumed at his own pathetic attempts to gain her interest. What does it take to tell me that I'm making a complete and utter fool out of myself, he raged. What am I, an idiot?

He berated himself all the way home, slamming the front door behind him with enough force to rattle the windows. Even an over large glass of whisky failed to calm his savage self-castigation and by the time he had climbed the stairs, slightly unsteadily after one drink too many, and thrown his tired body down onto his bed, his mind was too tightly wound to sleep. He could only lay staring with abject misery up at the moonlight slanting across the ceiling. Daniel made his mind up, that was it, he would give up. It was useless to pursue someone who clearly found him not to her taste. He gave a despairing groan. If only the heart was so easily persuaded.

At the same time, Zoe was also lying in bed staring up at her own ceiling, trying to make herself relax, but sleep continued to elude her. Something that had occurred with increasing regularity since meeting

Daniel. No matter how many times she changed the subject in her mind, his image would intrude and spoil her concentration. She was crying softly and steadily. Why was he so hard to forget? Why did the heart continue to harbour such painful emotions, when the mind could see more clearly that it was useless to go on pursuing that course. She sat up, disgusted with her own wayward thoughts, and slowly eased herself out of the bed. Feeling fragile and dejected, she wrapped her comfortable old dressing down snugly around her frozen body, and shuffled out into the kitchen to make herself a warm milky drink. She took it into the now chilly living room, flopping dejectedly down onto the couch and sipping her drink slowly, drawing comfort from its warmth. Picking a magazine up, she flicked through it in a desultory fashion, hoping to take her mind off that irritating man, but her eyes blurred as the tears continued to fall.

The next morning, after a miserable and restless night, Zoe was filled with a fresh determination to block Daniel right out of her life. She began to go out with Mike, taking him up on his offer of dinner and the occasional theatre trips. Then, as though to prove that she could, she encouraged the attentions of another man from work, who was more hopeful on the romance score than she had realised, and that bought her to her senses. She would stop trying to fill her life with meaningless company, It wasn't fair to them or herself. Mike was different. He was lonely for the same reasons and seemed more than happy with the occasional date. Gradually her days settled into a calm, if dull, routine.

ᘎᘎᘎᘎᘎᘎᘎᘎ

Libby seemed to be forever on the phone these days, murmuring sweet nothings to Jack, and Zoe had a job to get through to her. She could only assume that Jack must be paying. Libby's job couldn't possibly cover the expense of such frequent overseas calls, and she wondered how this long-distance romance could last when Jack worked with so many glamorous co-stars. It surprised Zoe that he had kept the contact up, and she had to give him credit for his persistence. It appeared that he thought more of Libby than she had imagined.

Jack had decided to come over and rent a place for the summer, and he had chosen a large, secluded house buried away in the countryside. It was surrounded by mature trees, with its own small stream running through the woods that thickly bordered one side of the garden. He had invited his parents over for a short stay and was going to take this opportunity to introduce Libby to them. The weather had been going through its usual unpredictable moods, but as luck would have it, the three weeks that he chose for his parents' visit stayed warm and sunny, so the large swimming pool was put to good use.

An invitation was also extended to Zoe and Tom to come down and join them, but she declined, feeling as though she would be intruding. Jack pressed her to accept, and with Libby's persuasion, she gave in, as she always did to her sister's blandishments. Tom drove them down and Zoe was now eagerly looking forward to the few days break from work. Especially as Libby had assured her that she could be safe in the knowledge that Daniel was not able to leave London at this present time, because of business commitments.

ᘎᘎᘎᘎᘎᘎᘎ

Zoe wasn't sure that she was going to like Jack's mother, Lorna, on first meeting her. She was a slightly neurotic woman, with sharp eyes, who hovered around her son possessively and studied Libby with a critical eye, as though finding her not quite to her taste. His father, Don, on the other hand, was a large genial handsome man, a complete contrast to his small wiry wife. Nevertheless, his mother tried her best to be friendly to them and after a few days, Zoe began to revise her opinion of Lorna Hammell. Yes, she was neurotic, and overprotective where her son was concerned, but she had every reason to be. In the world that Jack moved in were many pitfalls, and his mother had been there for him every step of the way on his journey to fame. Lorna had seen the disappointments and now the success. She knew, as Jack did, that this was a precarious stage in his life. Now she faced a new problem, a woman who her son professed to love, and her main worry was did this girl really love her son for himself, or his status. Was her love sincere?

Zoe was laying back on a lounger at the edge of the pool with her eyes closed. Even from here, she could hear Libby laughing and playing the fool with Jack inside the house, and smiled lazily to herself as she listened to their light-hearted antics. Suddenly a frisson of alarm coursed through her as she heard a deeper laugh joining in with theirs, and she sat up hastily, donning her sunglasses as though to hide herself. It couldn't be! He was supposed to be miles away, not here spoiling her tranquil holiday. If he was staying, she was leaving.

Libby came out, still smiling, and walked around the pool to Zoe's side, her face apologetic as she observed her sister's set expression.

"I thought you said that he was tied up in London and couldn't possibly get away," Zoe hissed.

"He was tied up," Libby protested. "I guess he managed to conduct his business sooner than we had anticipated."

Zoe was distracted and her eyes rounded as Daniel appeared accompanied by a man, equally as tall as himself and so much like him that it had to be his brother. "Who is that?" she whispered to Libby.

"His brother, Hal, as you've probably guessed," Libby said. "Nice looking man, isn't he?"

"Very," Zoe agreed, eyeing him appreciatively. He was not as dark as Daniel, his hair was brown and curly, but he had the same charming smile as the other two men. "Tell me that he hasn't got the same obnoxious nature as Daniel," Zoe said, turning to Libby. "He looks far too nice to be his brother."

"Honestly, Zoe," Libby gave a gurgle of laughter. "Daniel isn't that bad. Why do you insist on casting him in such a bad light?"

"I don't have to," Zoe replied, with a sniff. "He does that all by himself."

When she was introduced to Hal, she smiled sweetly up at him, aware of the silent man standing beside him, his face white with anger as she allowed her hand to be held far longer than necessary by his grinning brother. Hal had been apprised of the score as far as Daniel was concerned by Jack, and played up to Zoe for all he was worth.

Daniel was furious. How come she let his brother paw her like that, and Zoe was actually flirting back to Hal's stupidly obvious remarks. A sudden fear coursed through him, were they genuinely attracted to each other? The thought was unbearable, and his face became positively stony as he watched the carefree banter between the two.

After lunch, they all sat on the terrace, except Daniel, who swam up and down the pool, his powerful, bronzed body cutting through the water as though he were preparing for a race. All the time that Zoe was conversing with Hal, she found herself sneaking looks at Daniel, drawn to the sheer perfection of his hard muscled frame, her eyes following the bunched muscles of his thighs as he levered himself out of the pool, and her breathing became restricted. She watched as he towelled himself dry, his face troubled and thoughtful, and turned quickly away, flushing as his eyes turned in her direction.

During a lull in the conversation, while his brother was distracted by something Jack was saying, Daniel got up and moved over to Zoe. "Can we talk?"

"We are talking," she said, wishing that Hal would rescue her.

"I mean really talk." His face was strained and white. "Please, come indoors with me."

"I don't think so," Zoe said, with finality. "Let's not complicate matters."

She turned away as Hal joined them and deliberately ignored Daniel. He felt despair engulf him as he observed their interest in each other, and when he heard that they had arranged to go out for a drink that evening, his humiliation and dejection were complete. That evening while they were out, Daniel quietly packed up and left. His whole plan had been a disaster. He had never imagined that his own brother would step in and succeed where he had failed.

Zoe was surprised and relieved when Jack told her the next morning that Daniel had returned to London. Yet part of her grieved. At least while he'd been with them, she could feast her eyes upon him, forbidden food for her heart. Try as she may, she found it hard to gain back the relaxed mood that she'd been in before Daniel had shown his face and was only able to unwind when the holiday neared its end. When the time came around for the girls to leave, they had established a rapport with Jack's mother, who had found that Libby, although lively, was a reliable and likeable girl and she was sorry to see them go. Lorna watched the two young sisters as they left with Tom and Jack, who also had to get back to the set, her mind now settled. Jack had, it seemed, chosen wisely.

Zoe's light-hearted flirtation with Hal came to nothing. It had never meant anything to either of them. They had only met twice since their stay at Jack's house and then only in a friendly fashion. Hal had been a charming and attentive escort, and they enjoyed each other's company very much, but he'd only intended his stay to be a brief one. He had to get back to his business. Apparently, Hal had someone back home that he was romantically involved with, and when Zoe asked him about her, it was as if she had opened the floodgates to his love for this woman. Much to her amusement, Hal spent the entire time that he had left with her talking animatedly about the other girl. One thing she was grateful for was that it gave him no opening to discuss Daniel, although watching him while he talked was a little unnerving because of his strong likeness to his brother, which simply served to increase her unhappiness.

Chapter Ten

Back to normal, Zoe thought, as she sat and surveyed the new mounds of rubbish that seemed to have accumulated almost overnight in Tom's small living room. Now, for some obscure reason, he had decided to renew the cupboard doors and build a bookcase all at the same time. The doors had looked perfectly all right to her, but when Tom decided on a task, he couldn't be deterred. Zoe looked up as the front door opened and her brother came in.

"Good, you're still here." He held a small carrier bag up. "Chinese food! I thought you might fancy some."

"Mm, lovely." Zoe sniffed as the delicious aroma wafted towards her, suddenly realising how hungry she was. "I'll warm the plates and make coffee."

Over the meal, Tom casually mentioned that Jack was due back to see Libby in three days' time and would Zoe help him prepare a meal to celebrate his return, at her apartment of course, as it was more inviting. She stared at him, her heart jumping at the thought of Jack making another appearance. The problem with that was that Daniel usually accompanied him, and she simply couldn't handle seeing him at the moment.

"I don't know, Tom," Zoe said warily. "Libby is better at that sort of thing and anyway, her place is larger than mine."

"Yes, but she's so caught up with Jack that she would be a bundle of nerves, so it would be more convenient at your place, and they can leave when they like. Libby can hardly throw us out when Jack and her feel like a bit of smooching." Then he put in as an aside, "Oh, yes, and he's bringing someone with him."

At her panic-stricken face, Tom hastened to assure her that the person he was referring to was a woman. "I think she wants to meet Libby, see if she's suitable."

"Suitable." Zoe frowned, her hackles rising. "I thought his mother had already approved?"

"My words, not hers, just a figure of speech," Tom said. "Anyway, as Libby is otherwise occupied, you will have to do. So, you can help me plan the food."

"Gee, thanks." She glared at her brother, who grinned back in amusement. "Exactly who is this woman?"

"I don't know," her brother said vaguely. "I didn't ask, Sylvia something or other."

"Why do men always miss out on establishing the most important facts?" She tutted with vexation, then narrowed her eyes suspiciously. "Nobody else coming you forgot to mention, is there? If that awful cousin of his arrives, I shall walk out."

"Why?" her brother asked innocently.

Zoe gave him a fulminating look, knowing full well that by now Libby would have passed on all the gossip, and gathering her coat and purse up made for the door. She turned and gave him a haughty look. "I have got better things to do than sit amongst all this rubble discussing unpleasant subjects."

"Will you do the party food then?" his words hung in the air as the door slammed with a resounding thud. Hmm, Tom mused, something about that man bugs her, I shall have to find out more from Libby.

Although Jack was tired from his journey, he made time to call in at Daniel's house on his way to see Libby and found his cousin working late in his study.

"So, this Mike then, Libby tells me that her sister has been out with him quite a lot lately, even taken her home to see ma and pa," Jack said casually, turning and looking in the mirror, straightening his tie. He paused. "I don't know why I'm telling you all this, I don't suppose it interests you in the least."

He saw his cousin's stricken face reflected behind him in the mirror and slowly turned, a smile tugging at his lips. "Why do you look as though I've just torn your favourite teddy away from you?"

"Don't be so damn stupid," Daniel grunted. "Clear off and let me get on with some work."

"Hmm." Jack stood leaning against the door with his arms folded, watching his cousin fight his demons.

"What do you mean...Hmm?" Daniel snapped.

"Did I detect the sour note of jealousy?" Jack tilted his head. He whipped the door open and made a strategic withdrawal as his cousin picked up a heavy paperweight. "I'm going, I'm going," he yelled, as he slammed the door behind him, then stood grinning to himself. So, his cousin, the indestructible block of wood, had been toppled by one small fiery lumberjack, without an axe in sight.

When Jack had gone, Daniel slumped forward burying his head in his hands, more utterly dejected than he had ever felt. His life seemed to stretch before him like a black tunnel, empty and meaningless.

ᘓᘓᘓᘓᘓᘓᘓ

Libby had the grace to turn up, flushed and breathless, with Jack in tow and at least help with some of the last-minute preparation for the party. She was in the kitchen with her sister, slicing fruit and placing it neatly into small glass bowls.

"There is something incredibly satisfying about chopping up fruit, isn't there?" Zoe said fiercely as she sliced through a pineapple, imagining it to be Daniel's head. "Grr," she growled, as she chopped vigorously at the pieces.

"Steady on, we want cubes not mush," Libby giggled and added, "Besides, he can't feel a thing."

Zoe laughed at her sister's observation; she had known exactly who Zoe was venting her spleen on. "Am I that obvious?" she sighed, smiling at Libby.

"You are to me," her sister laughed.

Zoe was laying the food out on the table, admiring the colourful array, when to her horror Daniel arrived. She looked up in time to see him enter, his powerful figure framed in the doorway. The stupid lecture she had given herself about forgetting Daniel died a quick death the second she saw him. For a moment, she felt as though her heart would stop as she gazed greedily at him, and she despaired at her own treacherous response as her pulse raced, making her tremble. She desperately needed to escape, but she found it was easier to say that she would walk out than to actually do it. Her inherent good manners prevented her from making a scene in front of her family, so she stood rooted to the spot, and if her erstwhile brother had been within arm's length, she would have strangled him. Her eyes turned to Daniel's companion and her heart sank. The woman holding his arm so familiarly was the same elegant brunette who had been holding his hand so lovingly in the restaurant, and she was staring with intense interest straight back at her.

Zoe was distracted as her sister joined her. "Who is she? I thought that Janine was his woman of the moment," Libby asked. She put her hand to her mouth. "Oh, sorry, sis."

"Why be sorry? Daniel can see who he pleases, it's nothing to do with me," Zoe said vehemently. "Nothing at all."

Daniel's face was set and cold as he walked to their side with his attractive companion, having heard the tail end of her conversation. There was an uncomfortable silence broken as Tom strolled over, the amiable smile on his face fading as he gazed at the slender dark-haired woman hanging on to Daniel's arm. Before either man could speak, the woman stepped forward, putting her hand out.

"Hi, allow me to introduce myself, it appears that these two have lost their manners." She indicated the glowering figure of her cousin and a dumbstruck Tom. She gave the two girls a friendly smile. "I'm Sylvia Hammell."

Shock coursed through Zoe as she registered the name, she knew that the two men had no sisters, so who was this, Daniel's wife?

Libby was the first to recover, having had the same thought, and she took the proffered hand. "Hello, I'm Libby, this is my sister, Zoe, and that is our brother, Tom." She nodded her head towards the still tongue-tied man standing to one side of Daniel, gazing at Sylvia with a strange faraway expression.

"It's certainly a pleasure to meet you at last," Sylvia smiled. "Jack has told me so much about you all."

Zoe stared at her friendly face, wanting to hate her, but she was so nice and genuinely seemed pleased to meet them. She felt a surge of raw anger as she glanced at the man standing so still and silent beside Sylvia. How could Daniel behave in such a way. Here he was, next to his wife and a woman that he had made advances to, and he didn't seem the least fazed by that unsavoury fact. She was so angry and upset that she could hardly speak and was relieved when the telephone rang, giving her the chance to escape from his presence.

"The Blue beard, the absolute swine," she gritted, as she snatched the phone up.

"I'm not that bad," a voice protested from the receiver.

"Oh, sorry, Mike," Zoe gave a sighing laugh. "You're not capable of being that rotten."

"Do you fancy meeting for a drink?" Mike sounded lonely and in need of a friend.

"Woman trouble?" Zoe sympathised. "Why don't you come over and join the party, I could do with some moral support myself."

Mike was only too pleased to take up her up on the offer and accepted with alacrity. Zoe was still smiling as she put the phone down, and jumped as Daniel spoke from just behind her.

"Who was that?"

"None of your business." She didn't turn around; Zoe couldn't bring herself to look at him.

"A man?" he asked abruptly.

"As I pointed out," she said. "Nothing to do with you."

Zoe went to move away, but his hand closed around her arm. "No, don't walk away, talk to me, tell me what I'm supposed to have done. Why are you so antagonistic towards me?" Daniel pulled her around. "Look at me."

"I've seen you before, thanks, and I've got better things to do," she snapped. "Your conceit is appalling."

"What does that mean?" he asked in confusion, his green eyes darkening. "Why have you been avoiding me and why didn't you meet me?"

"I thought that you might be too worn out," Zoe replied sarcastically.

"What are you talking about?" His head whirled with all these cryptic utterings.

"Oh, for pity's sake, I'm not a fool," she said, her voice strained and angry. "I won't be used by any man."

"It's no good, I can't keep up with this conversation," Daniel rubbed his hand over his face. "I don't know what the hell you're going on about."

"That's because you're so vain and self-centred," Zoe raged, her voice wobbling dangerously. "Now go away, stop calling me and after this, please don't come here again."

Zoe wrenched her arm away and made for her sister's side, wishing that she had never consented to have them all here. She wanted to hide herself away until Daniel had departed. Seeing him again made her realise that her hunger for him had not abated one jot, and she couldn't bear to be near him like this, knowing that he belonged to someone else.

Daniel stood looking after her departing figure, his face white, eyes dull, feeling more miserable by the minute. Sylvia, on the far side of the room, was deep in conversation with Jack, but her eyes had been monitoring the small exchange, and she drew Jack's attention to the warring pair.

"What is going on here, Jack? He's quite desperate over her, and she's pretty much in the same state from what I've observed. Yet she won't give him the time of day."

"Poor old Daniel. It's strange, isn't it, seeing him at a loss for a change." Jack stared across at his cousin. "This isn't one of his business deals, or his usual sophisticated girlfriends, and he doesn't know how to handle it at all. I don't know what he's done to upset her...unless..."

"Go on," Sylvia said impatiently. "If you have some idea, then spill it."

"Janine," he stated succinctly, looking thoughtfully at his cousin.

"Right, Janine," she repeated slowly as enlightenment dawned. "If Zoe has seen her all over him, no wonder she treats him like a mangy cat."

"Dog," Jack corrected, smiling.

"Allow me to know which animal I prefer when it has got mange," she laughed. Sylvia gazed up at him, her smile fading as she narrowed her eyes. "What shall we do about that nuisance of a woman? What we need is another man, someone new for her to sink her teeth into."

"Oh, no, not me," Jack held his hands up in protest. "I'm not going down that road, besides I'm in deep with Libby."

"Don't be silly," Sylvia said, dismissively. "I wasn't referring to you."

"Why don't we just tell Zoe what the problem is," Jack asked. "That's the logical thing to do, seems straightforward to me."

"The way Janine can be with her poisoned barbs," Sylvia explained patiently. "Plus, the fact that she always seems to be at his side, who would you believe, if you didn't know him as we do."

"I take your point," he said slowly. "I can't help feeling sorry for Daniel, although in a way, it serves him right for tolerating Janine."

"I think that's on your account," Sylvia stated.

"How do you mean?" Jack asked in surprise.

"Daniel knows that she could cause a lot of trouble for you on set, if she was so minded," Sylvia explained. "You had no idea, did you? He's keeping her sweet."

"What possible trouble could she cause?" Jack scoffed.

"Please don't make me laugh, we're talking about Janine here," Sylvia snorted. "What about Roberto Mennella? His career took a nosedive after that trouble she caused at the Rome studio."

"Hmm, I see what you mean." His eyes widened in alarm as he remembered how the poor man's name had been plastered all over the national newspapers. It wasn't only his career that had suffered, so had his poor wife, and although memories faded, it had left an extremely bad taste behind. Some people still believed Janine's version of events.

"I'll think of something," his cousin said with determination.

"I bet you will," Jack laughed.

Zoe waited impatiently for Mike to arrive, rushing over to the door and opening it as soon as she heard the bell. "Hello, Mike, am I glad to see you," she said, grabbing his arm and pulling him inside.

"As grateful as I am for your amorous attentions," Mike smiled, "why do I get the impression that you have an ulterior motive?"

"I'm sorry," she laughed, squeezing his arm. "Am I that transparent?"

"Only to me. I gather the monster is here." He looked swiftly around, gulping as he encountered the hard stare from across the room.

"You guessed right," Zoe replied. "It's my turn to need a friend."

"I'm your man." He patted her arm. His voice trailed away as an icy glare from right behind her greeted his words. For a big man he sure moved fast.

Zoe glanced around, swallowing at the set furious look on Daniel's face, and Mike instinctively stepped back as the large man moved threateningly towards him. He was surprised as a hand was thrust out. He shook it gingerly, waiting for the crunch of bones that he was sure would follow, and was relieved when after a brief touch his hand was released.

"One of Zoe's friends?" Daniel enquired abruptly, baring his teeth in what passed as a smile.

"Very much so," beamed Mike, pushing his luck. "More than a friend, eh, gorgeous?" He slid an arm around Zoe's shoulders, giving her an affectionate hug.

Daniel glared at her pink cheeks and the arm draped casually around her, she was obviously happy to see this skinny man. He wasn't even good looking, he seethed, what the hell did she see in him. What had he got that Daniel himself seemed to lack?

"We must be off, darling," Zoe gushed, "if we want to see the last film."

"Huh? Oh, yeah," Mike enthused. "That one we were discussing. Sure, let's go, babe."

Zoe knew that her departure would be seen as rude, and she could see Libby's cross face looking accusingly at her as she left the flat, but she couldn't stand to stay in the same room with that insufferable man any longer. She just hoped that his poor wife hadn't noticed the angry expression on his face when he'd seen Zoe with Mike. What an awful man to be married to, it must be a nightmare. How could you ever trust him, and how did Sylvia deal with the constant presence of Janine in his life? The thought of him actually being married was something that Zoe couldn't even bear to think about.

Daniel was left fuming as the door shut behind the couple, then his anger drained away as despair engulfed him. She seemed very fond of this man, and by the familiar way they had greeted each other, had known him for some time. It seemed that he stood no chance with her, and the thought ate at him, filling him with unutterable sadness and frustration. He leaned listlessly against the wall, glass in hand, listening to the flow of conversation, wanting to go home, but he couldn't just rush Sylvia off. She wanted to get to know Libby, and Daniel couldn't leave her to make her way home alone, so he was forced to bide his time before he could make his escape.

ᘎᘎᘎᘎᘎᘎᘎ

Once the couple were outside, they were at a loss. Zoe suggested that they go back to Tom's place and have a drink, but Mike thought that it might cheer her up if he took her home to his parent's place. It would help to while away the time. His mother was a sunny-natured person, and one couldn't be in her presence for long before finding themselves being drawn into the warmth of her personality.

"Well, that was a short-lived party," he chortled.

"Sorry, Mike. I always seem to be apologising to you these days."

"No problem. Okay, let's go visit mum," he smiled.

Mike lived with his parents in a modest, semi-detached house, which was situated on a busy road not far from where Zoe herself lived. The roar of the traffic was deafening and yet in her own small apartment, a stone's throw away, the sound dwindled to a muted whisper. Even inside Mike's house, once the front door had closed behind them, the noise of traffic became forgotten as the cosy interior folded around them invitingly. Zoe felt relaxed and comfortable and very welcome in his home as his mother seemed inordinately pleased to see her. Probably because this was the second occasion he had brought her to meet his parents, and they thought that Mike had finally brought a girlfriend home at last. He winked at Zoe behind his mother's back. If it made her happy to think that, then let her, he implied. She shook her head at him, Zoe didn't want his mother to harbour any false illusions about her relationship to her son. If his mother was disappointed, she didn't show it, bustling about making them tea, insisting that Zoe stayed and ate with them, which she appreciated. She had been so intent on escaping that she hadn't eaten any of the food provided.

After an enjoyable, relaxing evening, Mike escorted her home, and they walked in companionable silence until they reached her flat. "I had a good time, Mike," Zoe said, smiling up at him. "Your parents are so nice; how did they produce someone like you?"

"Ah, but they think I'm wonderful," Mike laughed. "They don't see through to my darker side, as you do."

He declined her invitation for coffee as it was late, and he knew that all she really wanted was to be alone. "I can't come in, you'll only try and keep me there," he joked. "What would my mother say if I didn't come home straight away? She knows how long it takes me to walk here, and is watching the clock as I speak."

Zoe giggled, and reaching up, pressed a kiss to his cheek, thanking him once again for his support, then gave him a wave and went through the doors.

Chapter Eleven

Mike was still smiling as he strolled away, but the smile rapidly faded and the hair stood up on his neck as he glanced across the street and saw the tall shadowy figure staring fixedly across at Zoe's windows. Daniel appeared not to have noticed him. He hadn't moved and stood hands in pockets, his broad shoulders hunched, looking up at her window.

When Zoe's light came on, Mike was shocked to see the utter desolation etched on his face. That certainly didn't look like a man who was in love with anyone else. He began to wonder if Zoe had got her wires crossed in some way. He paused, debating whether to interfere or not, then casting doubt aside he turned back, crossed the road, and planted himself in front of the now aggressive looking Daniel.

"We're not an item, you know," he stated, looking up into the man's miserable, yet fierce eyes.

"Pardon?" Daniel blinked, as though he had not heard him right.

"You heard me," Mike said with an air of bravado, as the large man stepped towards him. He gave a small smile. "She loves you; I can't think why. Thinks that you want to add her to your harem."

"My what?"

"Janine, for starters, your constant shadow," Mike explained. "Then there is the little matter of who we had assumed to be your wife, Sylvia, but I guess from the way you're acting we've got that totally wrong."

"She's my cousin. As for Janine, she's just a damned nuisance," Daniel said slowly, staring at him in shock, his eyes lighting up with hope. He paused. "Why didn't Zoe just simply ask me about them?"

"Did you ask her to explain about me?" Mike enquired, raising one eyebrow.

"In a roundabout way, but I felt that I didn't have the right to question her too deeply." Daniel stopped abruptly and gave a rueful smile. "I'm as bad as Zoe, aren't I?"

"Worse," Mike laughed. "I had heard that you were an articulate man, but I've seen little evidence of it so far. You've not managed very well where she's concerned."

"Well, it's too late now." Daniel glanced up at her window, seeing the light go out. He shrugged unhappily. "I shan't disturb her tonight."

"You've disturbed her enough already," Mike said. "Once more won't count against you, go for it."

Giving Mike a brief nod of gratitude, Daniel strode across the road, ran up the stairs to Zoe's apartment, then rang the bell.

Zoe frowned as she heard the doorbell ring, then thinking it might be Mike having forgotten something he was going to tell her; she lifted her hand to open the door. Then stopped. At this time of night, it would be foolish in the extreme not to check first. It could be anybody standing right outside.

"Who is it?" her hesitant voice sounded from behind the closed door.

"It's Daniel, let me in, I need to talk to you."

She froze in shock, then backed away from the door, her hand on her heart. "Well, I don't need to talk to you, so go away." She could hear the anguish sounding in her own voice, and this show of weakness angered her. "Go home to your wife, or Janine, or any of the other multitude of women you've probably got stashed away."

"Don't be so bloody daft, woman," Daniel growled. "Let me in and I'll explain."

"If you don't go away," she hissed, "I'll call the police."

"I haven't got any other women," he yelled in frustration.

"Huh!" she scoffed. "The day I believe that is the day you become Tronicman, now go away."

Daniel stood staring at the door, gnashing his teeth. What was it about this woman? He was either wallowing in unrequited love or seething with rage, he must want his head examined. He stalked away, going over her words in his mind, and a slow smile formed on his face as he planned his next move.

Zoe leaned back against the door, sniffing, trying to stem the tears. The beast! There was poor Sylvia waiting for him at home and here he was, trying to gain access and climb into her bed. The awful thing was that she'd been very tempted to let him.

Zoe fumed as she slammed the phone down. How dare he phone her? He had rung incessantly over the last few days, but she wouldn't talk to him. Now she had stopped taking calls altogether in case she heard his disturbing voice. Then the phone became strangely silent. Why isn't he phoning me, Zoe thought contrarily. Probably gone on to someone else, somebody more accommodating. That thought upset her and made her shed even more tears.

Libby and Tom came round to see her, wondering why she hadn't been answering her phone.

"I've been trying to get in touch all week," Libby said crossly. "Jack has to go back to the States soon and I'm going with him."

Jack, apparently, was holding a small party at Daniel's London home for past crew members and of course, he expected Libby's family to attend.

"Please, Zoe, for me," Libby pleaded. "I might not be back for some time."

"Oh, Lib, are you sure that it's wise to go with him?" Zoe said worriedly, noticing the glow on her sister's face. "It's a long way from home if things go wrong."

"Jack loves me," Libby stated with conviction. "He wants to marry me."

"Marry you?" Zoe was shocked. "Has he actually said so?"

"Yes." Libby gave her a mock frown, "he actually asked me to marry him."

"Sorry," Zoe shook her head, "I don't mean to sound so incredulous."

"I know what you mean and don't think I haven't pinched myself in case it's all a dream." Libby smiled at her. She sobered and gave Zoe a steady look. "You're wondering how long it will last, aren't you?"

Zoe stared back at her, biting her lip, and wondering how best to answer. What could she say without sounding too critical? It was love for her sister that made her worry so much. Stars were known for their quick marriages and even faster divorces. She couldn't bear the thought of the heartache that could lay in store for Libby.

Tom, who wasn't known for deep thinking, suddenly chimed in. "It's a chance we all have to take, isn't it? No matter who you choose, or what walk of life you're in, it can all fall apart or last forever. If you love someone, that's the risk you take, isn't it?" He paused. "You just have to hope that their love is equal to yours."

"Wow! Thank you for your support," Libby said, staring at Tom as though she had never seen him before. "Since when did you start reading books with words in?"

"Ah!" he smiled, "There's more to me than just this handsome exterior."

"Words of wisdom from Tom," Zoe laughed at her brother's smug face. "A first, I do believe."

"Why do you two think so little of me?" Her brother grimaced, looking suitably crestfallen. "What did I ever do to you?"

"Tore my favourite teddy to pieces, hid my best shoes," Libby offered. "They were never found again, by the way."

"Burnt my fairy books, swapped my scooter for marbles." Zoe rubbed her chin thoughtfully. "Let me see, the list appears to be endless, should I go on?"

"Okay, okay," Tom put his hands up in surrender. "So, I committed a few crimes, you can't hold them against me forever."

"With each pearl of wisdom you emit," Zoe said solemnly, "I will erase one of your many sins."

"Gee, thanks," Tom grinned, then he frowned thoughtfully. "Anyway, how come you remembered all those misdeeds, I thought I'd covered my tracks fairly well?"

The two girls rolled their eyes at him and sighed gustily. "Honestly, Tom."

He laughed as he recalled those familiar words. They had been his sisters' recurring catchphrase whilst he'd been growing up, and he wondered if they knew just how many mischievous mishaps had been entirely down to him. Now, looking at their knowing faces, he could only conclude that they had always seen straight through his carefully manufactured excuses.

"Thanks, Tom," Zoe said, now serious. "I mean it, you were right about people taking a chance on love and I guess Libby has to take hers."

"Yes, thanks for your moral support." Libby squeezed his arm. She turned to Zoe. "Now, are you going to come to this party, or not?"

"I don't think that would be very wise. Besides, you'll have Tom, with mum and dad for moral support." She groaned at Libby's beseeching face. "Don't look at me like that, you know I can't stand it."

"Well, give in now then," her sister giggled. "It will save time."

Zoe weakly caved in and promised to attend even knowing that Daniel may be there. After all, it was his house and anyway, he would probably be surrounded by a horde of women. She laughed sadly to herself. The women were multiplying by the minute; even he couldn't have that many.

ᘔᘔᘔᘔᘔᘔᘔ

Zoe was determined not to go alone and as Tom seemed to have acquired a date, she once again enlisted Mike's help. He was only too happy to oblige and seemed excessively cheerful at the prospect, a fact that Zoe commented upon.

"Oh, you know," Mike blustered, "I don't get out that often. You never know, I might just meet my destiny at this bash."

She stared at him, her sixth sense telling her that there was more to the humorous twinkle in his eye than he was confessing, but as he was called away at that moment, she was unable to tackle him further on the subject.

Zoe was in a fluster on the day of the party, but she refused to go and buy a new dress. Why should she? After all, there was no one she wanted to impress. The result was that she tried everything on that she owned and then tried it all on again. She finally settled on the strappy dress that she'd worn to the last get together and made it look different by wearing delicate silver jewellery. She wore her hair up, darkened her make-up, and felt reasonably glamorous.

"Right, too bad if nobody likes it," Zoe said to her reflection. "I do."

"You look very nice, if I may say so," Mike offered when he came to collect her, and escorted her out to his car.

"Why thank you." She gave him the once over. "You look pretty good yourself. In fact, we make a very presentable couple."

"That's what you want, is it," he asked quietly, "to appear together as a couple?"

"I'm being pathetic again, aren't I?" Zoe looked at him, her face sad. "As if he would notice us."

"You might be surprised," Mike said softly, then on a brisker note as he helped her into the car, "Come on, we'd best get a move on, my girl, or Libby will think that you've changed your mind."

On the way to the party, Mike tried to explain about Sylvia and Janine, and where they fitted into Daniel's life. Zoe sank down in her seat as she listened and felt so embarrassed and upset about her treatment of Daniel that she ordered Mike to turn the car around and take her home.

"Why?" He stopped the car and turned to her.

"I can't face him," she wailed in despair, putting her head in her hands. "I've misjudged him so badly. What a fool he must think me."

"I don't believe he thinks that for one moment," Mike assured her. "Mad maybe, but no fool."

"Thanks," she murmured as she raised her head and dropped her hands. "I would still rather not go. I've embarrassed myself enough already."

"I'm not going to take you back home, you know." Mike glanced across at her with a gentle smile. "So, you'll just have to face him. Try talking to him, ask him about Janine."

"How can I? It's still none of my business," she sighed dolefully. "Despite all you say, Janine is still by his side, isn't she?"

"You're not listening, are you?" Mike said, a stirring of impatience in his voice. "It's you he wants."

"I know he wants me," Zoe said. "That's what frightens me. How long will it last?"

"Why don't you just go out with him and find out?" Mike heaved an annoyed sigh.

"Because I couldn't bear the pain when he finally tires of me." She gazed miserably at him. "Besides, look at me. There are far more glamorous women waiting in the wings."

"So why isn't he pursuing them?" he said in exasperation. "You really should stop comparing yourself to others. You are a very attractive girl, you know."

"Thank you," she said, with a faint smile. "Perhaps you're right, I will try talking to him, or rather listening for once."

"Good," he grinned. "Now onwards into the jaws of hell we go."

She laughed at his dramatic words, then sat quietly for the rest of the journey. Was her appeal for Daniel the very fact that she pushed him away? Were the others too easy? She sat in silent contemplation, wondering just how deep his feelings really were in regard to herself. She had thought that occasionally, apart from desire, she had glimpsed something needy and vulnerable in his eyes when he'd looked at her. Or was that just her own desperate longing, wanting to see her own emotion reflected in him.

The journey was all too short, and Zoe wondered if her palpitating heart was visible to Mike as she climbed from the car, but he made no comment as he held her trembling hand and they entered the open front door into the large hall. She walked in, her arm tucked through his, laughing at one of his awful jokes, when her attention was caught by the sudden hush that descended as they entered.

Everybody was looking up at the top of the wide, winding staircase and Zoe's mouth dropped open. There was Tronicman in all his splendour, every well-defined muscle lovingly outlined in the clinging blue suit, standing fists on hips head back, with arrogant jutting jaw gritted in warning that he was here to right a wrong, and her reaction was to laugh along with the others, which she did. Yet something seemed out of place. She frowned and cast a quick look around, wondering what it was that had troubled her conscience. Her gaze was caught by the good-looking couple standing slightly behind her, and realisation dawned. It was Jack, standing in evening dress beside her sister. Zoe's head whipped around again, and her eyes widened with shock as she looked back up at the large man and saw the green eyes gleaming down at her through the yellow mask.

"Oh, my..."

Zoe was bereft of words as he came bounding down the stairs, swept her up into his powerful arms, and threw her unceremoniously over his shoulder.

"Fear not, fair maiden! Do not despair. I have come to save you!"

Laughter erupted from the crowd around them as Zoe screamed, with a mixture of fright and soaring exhilaration, "Put me down, you big oaf."

Daniel strode towards the door, stopping just long enough to prise her fingers away from the frame. "Don't play hard to get," he admonished her. "Tronicman always gets his woman."

"For pity's sake," she spluttered, punching his back. "Put me down, people will talk."

"No problem," Daniel smirked as he carried her easily out on to the pavement and set her on her feet without fully releasing her. "My cousin will shoulder the blame; he's the real Tronicman, remember. The papers will have a field day, 'Superhero carries off squealing maiden.'"

"I am *not* squealing," Zoe protested, swatting feebly at his back.

"No, you're not, are you?" he said thoughtfully. "Shouldn't you be?"

"Let me handle shock in my own way," she said, trying not to laugh, but the delight and joy in her was bubbling up threatening to erupt.

Neither of them had noticed the bitter look that Janine threw them as she watched the pair leave. She was furious, the hard icy expression on her face not boding well for the couple. Janine stood talking, her face a mask of smiling politeness, but inside she was seething with rage and humiliation. She considered Daniel to be her property. He was exactly what she wanted, rich, well connected, and good looking, a perfect foil for her own beauty. Now that stupid little bitch had stolen him from under her nose. What possible attraction could the girl have for him; she was positively plain. Well, she would teach him a lesson he wouldn't forget. Daniel couldn't snub her like this and get away with it.

Daniel bundled Zoe into the car and drove as though his life depended on it, straight to her apartment. "Right, upstairs you," he commanded, as he hustled her up ahead of him, giving her no chance to escape. "We need to talk."

As soon as Zoe had closed the door behind them, he grabbed her and tore his mask off. "I'm furious with you," he said harshly as he pinned her up against the wall with his large body. "Angry." His head lowered, until his lips were a fraction away from hers. "Enraged." Daniel gave a despairing sigh as his mouth brushed her lips. "I have this desperate need to punish you."

Zoe's head fell back feebly as his lips parted her willing mouth, and he began a slow punishing assault on her senses.

"Are you feeling suitably sorry yet?" he murmured, drawing away slightly to let her breathe, his own chest heaving from their passionate caresses.

"No," she sighed, weakly. "I feel that I need to be taught a prolonged lesson."

"I can do that," he offered instantly. "Where's the bedroom?"

Zoe stiffened and pulled away slightly. So, a few kisses and he thought that led straight to the big seduction scene. "No, I am not one of your loose women that you can just pick up and put down when you please. You over-sexed chauvinist."

"Don't," he said hoarsely. "I can't bear you judging me like this. I really would have to be a superhero to keep up with all these mythical women that you've credited me with, especially when I love you so much." He framed her face with his hands, tenderly stroking the long blonde hair back from her forehead.

"What?!" Zoe gasped inelegantly.

"You heard," he whispered, moving suggestively against her. "For my sins, I am madly in love with you. I know that you don't feel quite the same, but I'll take what you care to give me, I'm that desperate. How's that for a complete loss of pride?"

"It may interest you to know," Zoe said softly, as she gazed up into his flushed face and observed the anxiety in his eyes which Daniel couldn't hide, "that I have loved and loathed you for a long time. The love may have just won out, I think."

Zoe tilted her head and smiled alluringly up at him, her smile faltering and her pulse racing as his mouth sought and found hers again in a mind-shattering kiss. As his body pressed strongly against hers, she felt panic invade, Daniel was so large and powerful.

"Oh, we mustn't... I don't," she mumbled incoherently against his marauding mouth.

It was hard to draw back, feeling so wound up, but Daniel eased off slightly, sensing her fear. "Okay, how about if I restrain myself until tomorrow?"

"Tomorrow?" Zoe echoed weakly, opening her eyes and gazing up at him in bewilderment.

"Yes," he breathed, brushing his lips gently over her forehead. "It's my birthday, and I've wanted a present like you for a very long time, so, my darling, we wait."

"Can you wait that long?" she whispered against his throat. Zoe felt her body relax as a laugh welled up.

"I can only try. Let's just touch and see how it goes," Daniel laughed huskily, his voice dying on a groan as he pushed her down onto the couch, trapping her beneath him.

Zoe felt a tremble of desire and amusement course through her body. Both of them knew that he wouldn't wait. His birthday present had arrived sooner than he thought, and she gave herself up to the unequal struggle with a sigh of surrender.

As it happened, they had to wait a little longer, because as Daniel's passion mounted, he became painfully aware of the restrictive pressure of the material encasing him. "Oh, God, help me out of this damn thing before I incur a life-changing injury," he pleaded, as he levered himself reluctantly away.

"I'm not sure if I should," Zoe laughed softly. "At least I know that I'm safe with you trapped inside those tights."

"Please," he murmured persuasively against her lips.

"If I must." She gave in weakly and helped him struggle out of the skintight garment, peeling it down his body, her eyes widening as his potent masculinity was exposed. Zoe felt the flush of heat that coursed through her, and a surge of desire as she gazed upon him.

"Stop cringing," Daniel said with a strained smile, his own churning emotions threatening to get out of control. "Conduct yourself like a true soldier."

"Very well," she sighed, her voice trembling. Completely surrendering and becoming boneless as his mouth closed over hers, moving softly, erotically, full of rich promise.

Daniel pulled the straps of her flimsy dress over her shoulders and slid it down, pulling it away from her body with an expertise that should have worried her, but didn't. Then he held her gently, running his large hands slowly down her ribcage, lowering his heavy weight carefully onto her suddenly pliant body. He leaned up on his elbows, pressing small kisses to her hot skin as she moved restlessly beneath him, feeling the raw hard power of his muscular body as it covered hers, insistently probing, seeking the comfort he sensed within.

Zoe was past caring now, completely incapable of any form of resistance. She needed him as desperately as he wanted her. Her arms were clamped around Daniel, clinging around his neck, and only slackening her grip as his mouth moved down, tracing a path to her aroused breasts, touching the tips with his tongue and teeth, until she began to writhe helplessly beneath him. Zoe could feel his hot swollen flesh against her leg and he smiled, pressing his lips against her skin as he felt her nervous tremble.

"Relax," he said softly. "I'm going to take it easy. I can, you know, despite what it feels like."

For the first time, Zoe became aware of the tremor that was shaking his own strong frame and the thought that she could be the cause of it made her melt against him.

His hand began a circular stroking movement as it travelled down her body. "First I explore stealthily," he said hoarsely as his hand moved more intimately on her. "Then, while my prey is lulled into a more amenable mood, I invade."

His voice became harsh and erratic as he pushed forward and began to enter her. He tried to stop as he met with resistance, but her soft body felt so good that sanity deserted him, and he continued thrusting into her, hearing her small sob in a corner of his mind as his body drove relentlessly on until he gained that mind-numbing release. His breath rattled in his throat as he collapsed onto her and tried to regain some remnant of control.

Daniel could feel her small hands stroking his back, as though he was the one who needed comfort. Groaning with remorse, he eased his heavy body away from hers. "You should have told me!" he said, guiltily. "Why didn't you stop me?"

"For the same reason that you couldn't stop doing what you did," she whispered shyly, raising tear-filled eyes to his, suddenly embarrassed by their naked, entwined bodies.

Daniel let his gaze wander and tensed as he saw the faint bruises on her thighs. "Oh, God, I'm sorry. I didn't mean to hurt you, honey. Christ, I'm a savage; I've never lost my head like this before." He looked down into her eyes anxiously. "You do believe that, don't you? I would never deliberately hurt you."

"I believe you," she said quietly, glancing up into his pained remorseful eyes.

Daniel lay beside her, stroking her shivering body gently, then he leaned over her and cupped her face tenderly in one large hand. "Shouldn't you have warned me about such an important fact?"

"What should I have said, 'Excuse me, I'm a virgin,'" she said shyly. "How was I to know that this was going to take place? Besides, it's not something that I go around broadcasting. I'm a bit of an oddity in this day and age."

"I suppose you are," Daniel mused, staring down at her. He kissed her reverently. "My vanity is flattered that you gave me the gift of being the first, and I hope the last. It was a privilege, one that I would like to repeat." Zoe blushed as she saw the hot desire in his eyes. "Now I've got to start all over again," he teased.

"Can you...? I mean... Oh!" She giggled nervously and her voice failed her as she felt him pressing against her once more.

"Try me," he whispered. "Let me show you what a pleasure it should really be." Then his mouth descended forcefully, opening hers as his hands began to explore and stroke, bringing her to a pinnacle of an ecstasy she hadn't thought possible. This time her body accepted his eagerly, meeting his long slow thrusts with arching movements of her own, until they both soared mindlessly into that dark space where they were aware of nothing but the explosive force between them.

They lay spent, exhausted, and totally happy. Zoe turned her head and found herself gazing into his penetrating green eyes.

Daniel's mouth widened in a lazy smile as he saw her blush. "I should think you would blush, you hussy, you. Really, Miss Burgess, the things you do." He laughed as her colour increased, and she closed her eyes in embarrassment.

"Don't look at me," Zoe begged softly.

"I like looking at you," He gathered her close against his side, "and don't be ashamed of what is a perfectly natural reaction. Personally, I can put up with this sort of exploration on your part for hours."

Daniel laughed again as she smacked his chest, then rolled her over onto her back, capturing her arms and holding them above her head. "Now what are you going to do?" he inquired with interest as he leered down at her.

Zoe didn't answer. Instead her body began to undulate sinuously under his, bringing a pained groan from his throat, and a small smile to her face.

She woke feeling warm and comfortable, feeling the large male body resting firmly against her side. Oh, my, he is real, this isn't some erotic dream. I've done the deed. She lifted her head and gazed shyly into his laughing eyes.

"Good morning," Daniel said huskily.

"Morning!" She was shocked out of her lethargy. "We've been here all night?" He threw his arm across his eyes and groaned. "What is it?" she asked anxiously, raising herself up on one elbow and leaning over him.

"Who brought me here?" he whispered. "People will talk."

"Talk?" she repeated foolishly.

"I don't know how you got me into this compromising position, and I can't believe you took advantage of me like this," Daniel said, in a low voice. "Now you must do the decent thing."

"What are you going on about?" She tried to move his heavy arm, her lips curving in an amused smile.

"You'll have to marry me now," he stated, moving his arm swiftly and clamping her hard to his body. "I won't have my name bandied about among all your female acquaintances, as if I were some sort of kept man."

She laughed into his eyes and then realised how seriously he was regarding her. "You really mean it?" she said in hushed tones.

"I really mean it, from here," he said, pressing her hand onto his heart. Then he kissed her, trying to put all his feelings into his caressing lips.

Zoe knew how much he meant those words; she could feel the tension in his body as he waited for her reply and her heart swelled with love for him. It was overawing to think that this large handsome man was so in love with her. She opened her eyes, taking in his strong face, his powerful body, so closely entwined with hers. He was an arrogant man in his bearing and manner with most people, yet she knew that, with her, he lost control and became weak. The power of that thought made her shiver.

"If I must marry someone," Zoe said slowly, as though debating the fact, "I suppose it might just as well be you."

He drew his head back and looked down at her. "You minx, are you teasing me?"

"I'm deadly serious," she said, putting her hands gently on his face. "Just you try backing out of it."

"You couldn't make me," Daniel promised.

After much tussling, Zoe managed to extricate herself from Daniel's clutching arms and escape into the bathroom. She felt somewhat battered and bruised, but it was a pleasurable pain. She smiled reminiscently as she towelled herself down. When she came out, Daniel was still lying where she had left him and patted the couch invitingly.

"I think not," she protested. "Some of us have to go to work."

"Take the day off," he said persuasively. "Spend it with me."

Zoe threw his clothes at him and pointed at the bathroom, backing warily away as he stood up.

"Don't worry, I'll behave," he promised. "Even I run out of stamina now and then."

"You do surprise me," she giggled when Daniel sidled around her as if she might pounce on him.

"Strangely enough, I feel my strength returning," he said thoughtfully, pausing at the door.

"Go," she ordered.

"You are a hard woman," he grumbled, as he obediently disappeared into the bathroom.

While Daniel showered, Zoe made them toast and coffee. She had already phoned into work and made her excuses, anticipating the day ahead. They were both blissfully unaware that it was not going to turn out quite as planned.

Daniel sniffed appreciatively as he appeared again and smelt the coffee, but couldn't resist pulling Zoe into his arms once more.

As she recovered from his prolonged and satisfying kiss, she glanced down at the cushions scattered off her couch. "How did we manage with something so small?"

"That's real cruel, honey," Daniel said in a wounded voice.

"I meant the couch," she giggled.

"I love you; you do know that, don't you?" Daniel smiled, gazing intently at her, and holding her tightly.

"Yes, I know you do," she assured him, putting her arms around his waist, feeling her love well up. It made her want to cry to think that he was so unsure of himself where she was concerned. "The sooner I marry you the better, in case you decide that this was entrapment," she said.

"I don't mind being trapped by you." Daniel pressed his mouth against hers. "Now, let's go and tell my cousin that Tronicman has got his girl. I'll bet they're biting their fingernails."

"Did Mike know about this?" she asked suspiciously.

"Of course," he said smugly. "So did everybody else gathered at the house. They knew what a desperate man I had become."

It took Zoe another half an hour to soothe and console him.

Chapter Twelve

On their way over to his house, where Jack was now staying, Daniel tried to explain the situation with Janine. "When I first agreed to Sylvia's suggestion to try and distract her from pursuing Jack, neither of us had any real idea if it would make any difference. Unfortunately, the plan worked rather too well, and she transferred her attentions to me, deciding that I was the next best thing. She has been nothing but trouble ever since. She's like a leech, clinging on where she isn't wanted," he shrugged awkwardly. "I can't seem to get it into her head that I'm not available."

"You weren't even tempted, not once?" Zoe asked, lightly.

"Never! Not my type," he smiled, looking down at her with knowing eyes. "I like women with acid tongues who fight me over every move I make, and behold, I met one. I find I have now become addicted to verbal swordplay. The romantic side isn't bad either."

She laughed across at him. "You silver tongued flatterer!"

Daniel chuckled. "Want me to show you that I am more than a man of few words?"

"Not while you're driving," she pointed out.

He just gave her a warm sensual smile, which sent her pulses racing.

"Janine isn't going to be so happy when she hears about us, is she?" Zoe said worriedly.

"The party and my Tronicman stunt should have made it quite plain to her where my true feelings lie," he said grimly. "Janine would have to be particularly obtuse not to have taken it on board."

"I still feel a little uncomfortable where she's concerned," she said anxiously. "Janine really seemed to act as though she had some claim on you, imaginary or not."

"She'd better not try and cause trouble, or hurt you in any way," Daniel gritted, his brows lowering in a frown. He turned his head, his eyes dark with love and anger as he glanced down at her. "Janine will have me to answer to if she does."

Zoe stared at him, seeing the strength in his steely gaze as he glanced back at the road, and felt sorry for anyone who got in the way of such a man.

ᘎᘎᘎᘎᘎᘎᘎ

Daniel stood in front of his own front door and lifted his hand to ring the bell. "Why don't you use your key?" Zoe questioned.

"This is just to give them due warning, you never know what those two are up to," he smiled, but before he pressed it, he leaned over her and gave her a lingering kiss.

"What was that for?" she breathed. "Not that I'm complaining."

"So that you won't forget me, not for one moment," he said, running his hands over her hips.

"As if I could," Zoe sighed, nearly passing out as his hands tightened.

When the door opened, the first thing they were confronted with was Jack's furious face. He was waving a crushed newspaper in his fist, almost speechless with rage. He thrust the paper at Daniel, who tried unsuccessfully to straighten it out as they walked in.

"I can't read this, you've massacred it," he pointed out.

"Janine!" Jack sounded as though he were being strangled. "That stupid bloody woman has announced her engagement. It's in all the newspapers!"

"And?" Daniel queried, raising his brows.

"It's to me!" Jack rasped. "Why me, when it's obviously you that she wants? Now the press are having a field day and camping out at my hotel."

Daniel grabbed the paper and straightened it out as best he could, rapidly reading through the offending item. It made much of Janine's friendship with him, and how Jack had consoled her over his hurtful rejection, resulting in this sudden romantic engagement. She had found her true love at last.

"The spiteful bitch, choosing you gained her the utmost publicity," Daniel said angrily. "It's to get back at me, to spoil my life, whatever it takes, even if it means using you. How could they believe such arrant nonsense?"

Zoe stared at Libby, who was hovering anxiously behind Jack with her hands clasped. They exchanged frightened glances; was this the start of everything going wrong?

"You," Daniel said, sternly, holding Zoe gently by the shoulders. "Stay here, I'm going to pay Miss Mouth-Almighty an extremely unfriendly visit."

"Let me come with you, Daniel, and support you." She clutched at his arms. "Show her that we are a definite item."

He wanted to say no, but Daniel knew that Zoe needed to see him get Janine out of his life once and for all, and he couldn't blame her for this lapse of faith. He would have felt the same had it been the other way around.

They stayed just long enough to share a meal with the worried couple and then set off for London. In his haste to get there, Daniel did not disregard the speed restrictions as much as push them to the limit. He wanted to get this confrontation over with as soon as possible. He didn't like unpleasantness any more than Zoe did.

Janine was staying at one of the more prestigious hotels, which was strategically placed, in her view, to make her more visible to the media. It was also, much to Daniel's irritation, just a short walk from his own office block which made it far too easy for her to waylay him. His colleagues envied him, of course, being pursued by a glamorous star appeared to be no hardship, and any one of them would have exchanged places with him in a flash if they could. He sighed with irritation at the whole uncomfortable situation that Janine had managed to create, and looked across at Zoe sitting silently beside him. She was worth so much more than the other woman. In his eyes there was no comparison, and he would spend his life proving his love to her.

"I love you," he said softly, resting his hand reassuringly on hers. "Remember that, whatever Janine spits at you."

"How difficult will she be?" Zoe looked back at him with a worried frown on her face and gave a small nervous smile. "Should I prepare myself for battle?"

"If Janine tries anything vicious," Daniel growled. "She will have me to answer to and I certainly won't be pulling any punches."

She stared at his set face and was glad that she wasn't the one on the receiving end of that anger. He looked formidable, and Daniel was right; he would make a very bad enemy. She smiled to herself as she remembered his threat to her and how short-lived it had been. A few tears had destroyed his defences, but she had a strong hunch that the same ploy wouldn't work quite so well for Janine.

They confronted the actress at her luxury hotel, her smile of welcome dying as she opened the door and saw Zoe standing next to Daniel. "What is she doing here?" Janine asked petulantly. "How did you manage to get through the press?"

"Zoe is here because I need her to be," he said coldly. "I want her to hear what I have to say. As for the press, that was easy. I happen to know the manager of this hotel. We used the staff entrance."

"I might not wish to listen to anything you say," the actress cried in a shrill voice, faltering as he moved aggressively towards her, his face dark with anger. Janine stared up at him, her eyes wide with fear. She had never seen him like this before. Gone was the polite and smiling escort she thought she knew so well. In his place stood this coldly condemning man, and she was petrified. He was towering over her as if he would like to crush her between those large powerful hands.

"You will retract your ridiculous statement," Daniel stated icily, "or I, personally, will have great pleasure in tearing you into tiny pieces and feeding you bit by bit to the press."

"Telling them precisely what?" she sneered defiantly.

"Every juicy detail, all that I know, which as it happens is quite a substantial amount." He gave her a shark-like smile. "On the way over I compiled quite a fat dossier on you. A few strategic telephone calls to people who owe me favours, the list grew longer by the minute. Strangely enough, mostly information about that unpleasant incident in Rome."

Her face blanched when he mentioned Rome, and her capacity for speech seemed to desert her as she visualised her name and face in all the national newspapers. She knew that it would hardly be in a favourable light. "What shall I do?" Janine stammered weakly, her face white and pinched, making her look old.

"You will do as I instruct you to do," he warned grimly, not moved by her visible distress.

Zoe, standing as a silent witness to this scene, felt awful. She knew that Janine deserved being put in her place, yet she looked almost pathetic as she pleaded with Daniel. She herself would have hated to have had a witness to such humiliation. Zoe let herself out quietly, not wanting to see more, and waited outside in the car for Daniel to finish. It was some while before he appeared, breathing hard. When he eventually climbed into the car beside her, Daniel sat gripping the steering wheel, trying to calm his temper. He turned his head giving her a faint smile.

"I believe that Janine has finally got the message. She won't be bothering us again after tomorrow."

"How can you be so sure?" Zoe gazed across at him anxiously.

"Blackmail is an ugly word, one that I'm loath to use, but she now knows that I hold a good deal of unsavoury information about her. Things that I wouldn't hesitate to use if she plagues me or mine again." He sighed. The worry on her face made him want to reassure her. "Believe me when I say it would only be as a last resort that I would ever reveal her misdeeds, and there are plenty of them. It's amazing what depths some people will sink to just to reach the top. Hopefully I should never have the need to use the information."

Daniel had arranged for Janine, Jack, and himself, to attend a press gathering at his cousin's hotel and he wanted Libby and Zoe to be there with them.

"It will be a bit overwhelming for you both, but the good thing is that we will dispose of Janine once and for all. If the truth came out, she would be lucky to come out of this with any career left at all, but for now she can glory in the limelight, her reputation intact. The downside is the publicity for you two, but it had to happen sometime. People will want to know all about the girl who Jack is going to marry," Daniel told the girls. He smiled sympathetically at Libby. "You'll have to get used to the media after this fiasco, I'm afraid."

"It won't matter to me, as long as I'm safe with Jack." She shrugged and sighed. "All that trouble you and Zoe went to trying to throw the press off the scent, all wasted."

When the press were assembled in the lobby of the hotel, Daniel escorted Janine from the elevator, his cousin following closely, with Zoe and her sister walking reluctantly behind them. Daniel stood, his arm firmly around Janine's shoulders and faced the media. He explained how she had foiled the attempts of one particularly persistent fan by posing as Jack's fiancée for a short while.

"Janine did it out of her friendship for my cousin, to shield him from unwelcome advances, which were potentially dangerous. The case is now in the hands of our lawyers. As for us two, we never were an item, were we?" He smiled down at her, his eyes stony. "Now she wishes to set the record straight, isn't that right, Janine?"

"Yes." Janine fluttered her hands as she flicked her eyes nervously up at him. She turned her best melting wide eyed look on the assembled news hounds, who scrambled to take close ups of her pouting lips and generous cleavage. "That's right, I thought to protect him. You know, a smokescreen," Janine said, breathily as she posed seductively.

"Out of her generosity of heart," Daniel added, smiling at the reporters. "Now let me introduce you to his real fiancée."

It was like a rugby scrum as the reporters surged around the now blushing Libby, held closely against Jack's side. Most were thinking, good, a human-interest story, makes good reading. Only one journalist stood regarding Daniel and Janine with a speculative eye. The men were too busy focusing on her curves, but Molly Courtney, like all women, had seen something off in the story. She had noticed the swiftly masked anger on the man's face and knew that with a little more delving, she may just get some more information on Miss Snow White. She stared at Janine's pale face; all was not as it appeared, and the journalist was aching for a chance to get her own back on the star. She had been on the receiving end more than once of Janine's acid tongue. Male reporters were, of course, never shown that side of her, but they soon would be if Molly gained access to the true facts. It seemed that Janine would be punished by the press anyway, despite her polished performance.

Before they left the hotel, Daniel turned back and stood in the doorway of the room, looking down at Janine's defeated figure as she slumped in a chair. "I have tolerated you so far as a damned nuisance, but if you ever threaten my family again, I will make you pay big-time," he whispered in a deadly voice, which frightened her even more than his earlier more obvious anger.

ꟷꟷꟷ

When Daniel left her after a lingering good night, Zoe walked dazedly into her apartment. This had been quite a day, and she was tired, not to mention slightly stiff. She wandered into the shower, a dreamy smile on her face as she remembered what had caused the faint marks she saw as she washed herself down. She had never acted so irresponsibly in her life before, had never given herself fully like that, yet with Daniel she had cast her inhibitions to the wind, letting him take her without even a struggle and she had relished it. There had been fear and just a little pain, but that had soon been obliterated by the multitude of emotions that had swamped her, and she knew that Daniel had experienced the same loss of control. She gave a faint laugh as she recalled the glazed look on his face when she had, at one point, taken command.

Zoe stirred herself; if she carried on at this rate, she wouldn't be able to sleep at all. It was her day off tomorrow and in the morning, Tom's flat would have to be tackled again. Sometimes she wondered why she bothered; her brother should cope with the mess himself. I guess it's just force of habit, she thought fondly, always watching out for him like this. She pondered on the thought of another woman taking her brother on. Would she and her sister feel a twinge of jealousy if such a determined female took their place? Nah! She gave an amused laugh at such an absurd thought. Why would she worry over that when she had Daniel? She had a feeling that he would monopolise all her time in many and varied ways. Zoe blushed as her mind began to wander off at a tangent again.

When she finally arrived at Tom's, it was nearly lunchtime, her own wayward thoughts having made her toss and turn, keeping her awake most of the night, with the result that she was later than usual. She was also soaking wet, the heavens waiting until she had stepped outside before pouring their contents all over her. So now her hair and clothes dripped uncomfortably, and she wasted time trying to find a clean towel to dry her hair. Now she would have to rush around to clear a space in the rubbish before she could even begin to tidy up properly. Sometime later, when Libby let herself into the flat, she found Zoe sitting on a stool staring dreamily out of the window surrounded by cleaning equipment, her rubber-gloved hands laying idly in her lap.

"I know the rain running down the window must be absolutely riveting," Libby's voice penetrated her thoughts, her hand waving up and down in front of Zoe's face, trying to break her out of her trance. "Please tell me that there's something else on your mind, or should I start worrying about your fragile mental state?"

"I gave in." Zoe sighed, turning soulful eyes to her sister.

"What?" Libby gasped, knowing exactly what her sister was referring to. She also knew that this was the first time that her sister had ever really been intimate with a man and although she herself was no innocent, was still stunned. And Libby also knew just how overpowering the cousins could be; one was dealing with potent masculinity here. She found herself identifying with Zoe's concern over her own past escapades.

"I don't know why I'm so shocked," Libby said, apologetically. "I mean it was pretty obvious that something had happened when neither of you came back all night." She sank down on the seat opposite her sister and stared at her apprehensively. "Are you okay?"

"I think so," Zoe gulped, her voice rising to a wail as she returned the look, her eyes swimming with tears. "He says that he loves me and wants to marry me."

"So why are you crying?"

"I don't know," Zoe sniffed. "I love Daniel so much that I can't stop thinking about him and I feel as though it's too good to be true."

"Don't start doubting him now," Libby said sternly. "You'll break his heart. I know for a fact that he is totally smitten with you, desperately so, if Jack is to be believed."

She laughed as Zoe said slowly, "Really, smitten with me? I like that, it sounds good."

Tom came in as they were whispering over coffee, noting with concern Zoe wiping her red eyes. "What's up, sis?" He hovered over her, his eyes narrowing. "Somebody done something to upset you?"

This was yet another facet of Tom's nature that they had not seen in him before, he sounded aggressive and protective. "Why, Tom, I didn't know you cared," Zoe said lightly, drying her eyes.

"Don't joke," he warned. "Tell me what's wrong."

"I'm in love."

"Then why are you crying?" He raised his brows in bewilderment.

"That's precisely what Libby said," she giggled, giving him a watery smile. "Take no notice of me, I'm a bit touchy at the moment. Love does that, you know."

"Well, thank God I'm not in love," Tom snorted, "If that's what it makes you degenerate into, a snivelling wreck." He skipped backwards, her punch missing him by inches, laughing at her mock anger. Then he turned to more important matters, opening the refrigerator and searching around inside, seeking nourishment.

"Stop rummaging," Zoe scolded. "Your lunch is over here on the table."

She sat and watched him demolish his food in record time, wondering about his own feelings where Sylvia was concerned. Both sisters had noticed the struck look on his face when he had first met Daniel's cousin. He may mock love, but he was not, it seemed, immune to it. With Libby's help, they made short work of the cleaning, and Zoe made tiredly for home.

As she let herself in, the phone rang. It was Daniel. "I have to work late," he apologised. "Come up to town, meet me after work about eight. The place will be closed, so just tap on the door and John on the security desk will open it for you. We can go out for a meal afterwards."

The rest of the day seemed to drag on as Zoe waited for the time to leave and she couldn't seem to concentrate on her allotted tasks, her thoughts continually straying to Daniel. She remembered the last time she'd entered his office, and the misery that she'd caused both of them by her misinterpretation of the scene taking place. Mind you, she thought dreamily, it had been enormous fun making up. She found herself blushing at the erotic images her mind was conjuring up and laughed softly as she put her work carefully away in preparation to leave.

She sat staring vacantly out of the train window as it rattled noisily on towards her destination. It seemed to be taking forever, and she was grateful when it finally pulled into the station. The building was dark when she approached it, but for a small light illuminating the back of the foyer. Zoe pressed her face against the glass and peered in, giving a tentative tap on the door. Almost immediately a burly security guard appeared, his eyes narrowed suspiciously, but when she uttered Daniel's name, a magical transformation took place. His face crinkled into a friendly smile, and he partially opened the door, letting her slide in before locking it firmly behind her. He ushered her into the elevator, giving her another polite smile as he leaned in and pressed the button that would take her up to Daniel's floor. "Sorry I can't come up with you," he apologised. "I hope that you understand, I'm not allowed to leave my post."

"Don't worry," she smiled. "I know my way."

"It's just that this place can be a bit overwhelming in the subdued lighting at night." He looked concerned.

"Mr Hammell will meet me at the elevator," Zoe reassured him. "Perhaps you could just give him a buzz and let him know that I'm on my way up."

The security guard stood and watched as she was whisked away, then gave his boss a quick call.

As the doors opened, Daniel plucked her out of the elevator as if his life depended on it, crushing her against him and giving her a deep satisfying kiss. "I didn't know that I could miss you so much," he sighed. "How long have we been apart?"

"Not long," she laughed. "Now put me down and finish what you have to do, or we'll never get to the restaurant, and I'm hungry."

She sat listening to the silence, only disturbed by Daniel's quiet breathing as he looked at the sheets of paper and the computer in front of him with deep concentration. Every now and then, scribbling a brief memo on a notepad.

"It's no good," he said decisively, throwing his pen down. "I have to kiss them."

"What?" She asked nervously, jumping at his sudden movement.

"Your bruises," Daniel said, gazing at her mouth.

"But I've got them all over my body," she stated, unthinkingly.

"I know," he said wickedly, his eyes darkening with desire.

"Don't be silly," Zoe laughed, jumping to her feet and backing towards the door as he stood up. She turned around and grabbed the handle, but she was far too slow.

"It's a big desk." He indicated the large empty desk against the far wall.

"Daniel, we can't," she moaned as she felt his body harden against hers. "Not here."

"Who can't?" Daniel challenged her, his hands sliding her skirt up as he manoeuvred her over to the desk, laying her down on the surface. His hands arranging her skilfully to accommodate him.

He moved powerfully against her, burying himself in her velvet softness, trying to restrain his desire, but as her body helplessly responded, his hard-held control snapped and Daniel surged urgently into her, casting them both out into that same deep, dark pool.

Rendering them totally mindless for what seemed an eternity yet lasted only minutes. He collapsed over her, breathing hard, shocked at his own loss of control. "I'm an animal," he groaned against her throat.

"I know, I've got the bruises to prove it," Zoe smiled wearily. She whimpered as his hand settled more intimately between them and began to wander. "Oh, I thought you were finished!"

"Not quite," Daniel said huskily, as he began a soul-destroying exploration of her most vulnerable regions. As her body reached fulfilment and convulsed against his, he thrust into her once again, moving slowly, sensuously, giving her the utmost pleasure as he continued his gentle onslaught.

They lay together waiting for their pounding hearts to still, and Daniel lifted his head reluctantly. "I shall never think of my desk in the same way again." He raised himself up on his arms, gazing down at her blonde hair, fanned out like trails of silk across the surface.

"I like your desk." She smiled up at him and let her hand slide lovingly over the surface of the polished wood that she lay on. "So smooth and shiny."

"Stop that," he commanded. "Don't make me jealous of my own furniture. If you want to stroke something, choose me, I'm available." He pressed down on her and laughed as she slapped at his arms, trying to free herself. "Okay, I get the message, Oddly enough, I feel quite tired, as well."

As they straightened their clothing, Zoe felt suddenly shy and blushed as she caught his eyes watching her smooth her skirt down.

"Come on," he growled. "Let's go home."

"I thought we were going for a meal," she protested, as he took her arm in a firm grip.

"Self, self, self," he grumbled. "Come on, I'll make you a sandwich."

"Please, don't spoil me," Zoe begged sarcastically.

"Okay," Daniel agreed amiably. "Straight to bed it is."

Zoe was still laughing helplessly as he bundled her into the car with undignified haste.

The next morning when Jack walked into the office leaving a trail of swooning women behind him, he found Daniel, head bent, seated at his spare desk looking at it as though mesmerised.

"What's so interesting about your desk?" Jack stared at him with a puzzled frown.

"You'd be surprised." Daniel raised his eyes dreamily, then sat up straight as he became aware of where he was, and who he was talking to. He cleared his throat. "Sorry, did you want something?"

Jack watched the flush that invaded his cousin's face with fascination, and grinned. "Something I should know about?"

"Mind your own business," Daniel snapped irritably.

"Hmm," Jack murmured, what would he do if he got Libby alone in here. His eyes did a quick scan of the room. "Ah!" His face lit with understanding, and he gave the other man a devilish grin.

"Don't you say one word," his cousin warned, his eyes narrowing dangerously as he saw where Jack's gaze had rested.

"That's okay, I understand," Jack said conspiratorially. "You have a desk fetish, perfectly normal." He ducked as his cousin flicked his pen at him and backed away in mock fear.

"Tell me what you want," Daniel warned, "or clear off and don't come back."

"Take it easy, big guy. Libby and I are having lunch at your favourite restaurant," Jack laughed as he saw the grin forming on Daniel's face. He turned to the door and added cunningly. "I thought you might like to meet up, 12:30. Zoe will be there."

"Let me get on with some work, you devious superhero," Daniel growled, adding casually, "I might meet you, or I might not. It depends if I can find the time."

Jack sauntered out of the office, smiling to himself, completely unaware of the commotion his presence had caused among the female staff. Even Margaret wished she were a little younger as she watched his panther-like movements when he strode past her desk and entered the elevator.

Chapter Thirteen

Daniel was the first to arrive at the restaurant and when Zoe entered, she faltered at the look on his face. He had been watching out for her arrival, and his eyes fixed on her as though he were drowning. That vulnerable look made her rush to the table and leaning down, she planted a lingering urgent kiss onto his mouth, feeling his instant passionate response.

"Have you been waiting long?" she asked, sliding into the seat beside him.

"All my life," he murmured huskily.

Zoe blushed at the fervour in his voice and fanned herself with the menu. "You make me hot."

"Likewise," he murmured.

She felt the exploring hand travelling up her leg and smacked it hard.

"Ow! You hurt me," he whined plaintively, as he looked at the red mark that she had inflicted and hunched over, nursing his hand.

"Serves you right," she giggled. "You lecherous beast."

"You know you love me, really." Daniel smiled at her, his eyes twinkling. "Even with all my faults, and before you say anything, yes, I know I have many."

Zoe gazed at this handsome man who had stolen her heart with such love in her eyes that his breath almost stopped.

"Don't look at me like that," he pleaded. "You don't know what it does to me."

"Yes, I do," she said softly, the same helpless emotion reflected in her own eyes.

"Do we have to eat," he groaned. "Can't we just go home?"

"There are two appetites, and this one has to be fed, as well," she reminded him. "Anyway, we're supposed to be waiting for Jack and Libby."

"We could stand them up," Daniel suggested, with a wicked smile. He sat and watched as she sipped her wine, noticing how her soft lips retained a drop of moisture and moved his chair nearer. "You have something on your lips," he whispered.

"What is it?" Zoe asked, putting her napkin up to her mouth. As her lips parted, his descended and took hers in a quick, hard kiss. "You sneak," she gurgled, trying not to encourage him. Her laughter drained away at the smouldering look in his eyes. He took advantage of the moment and once again his lips claimed hers in a prolonged draining kiss. "Daniel, will you please behave," she pleaded, her face hot as she gazed helplessly at him, her own pulse clamouring.

"I can't help it," he said hoarsely. "You bring out my worst behaviour."

"That's right, blame me." She gave him such a seductive smile that it made him groan and snatch her hand up, pressing it to his mouth. Zoe gave a gasp of smothered laughter as he nibbled her fingers. "Will you please stop that? People are looking."

"That's because they wish they could nibble on them too." He grinned, and looking around, found himself gazing into the eyes of one of his colleagues. For a moment Daniel froze, then gave a final nip. So what if the man saw him playing the fool? It wouldn't be the first time. Lately his colleagues must have thought that he was heading for some sort of breakdown and no doubt the man was wondering why he was seated at a table with the same demented woman who had stormed into his office. Daniel smiled as the man grinned at him and winked.

"I saw that," Zoe accused him. "What was that supposed to mean?"

"Ah!" he smirked. "Just a man thing. He now knows that I have completely flipped over a domineering woman."

She laughed and caressed his hand, rubbing her thumb over his wrist.

"Don't tempt fate," he warned her, moving nearer. Fortunately, at that moment, Jack and Libby appeared.

Libby laughed as they approached the table and Daniel held his hand up pathetically, pointing to the red mark.

"Just what have you been up to?" Jack smiled. "Nothing good I'll bet."

The meal was an enjoyable affair. Libby and Jack had decided to get married quietly in two weeks' time and then embark for America. Now Daniel was insisting on a date for their own wedding.

Zoe gazed at him, her eyes soft, imagining him as her husband. She laughed to herself; he would hardly be docile. If she married him, she would have to wage a permanent war to retain her own personality, but then she had always loved a challenge. She eyed him as he glanced at her, his green eyes gleaming, waiting for her answer. "Name a day," she dared him. "I'll be there."

Daniel was taken aback and sat without speaking as he digested her words.

Libby laughed and clapped her hands, exclaiming gleefully, "At last! Come on, Daniel, answer, or we'll think that it was just false promises on your part."

"If I must," he grumbled, screwing his eyes up as though wondering if he should commit himself, then he said. "Today."

"Don't be silly, Daniel." Zoe gave a gasp of laughter.

"I'm serious." He gazed at her solemnly. "I thought you liked a challenge."

"I do," she said tremulously. "You've taken me by surprise, that's all. I don't think that we can get married just like that, can we?"

"Really, Daniel, let my poor sister gather her wits," Libby beseeched him, coming to her rescue. "At least let her have time to prepare for such a momentous occasion."

"Zoe is the one who said name the day," Daniel protested, then relented, saying with a smile, "Okay, make it four weeks, which will give us both plenty of time to rearrange our work schedules."

Daniel was fully aware of the start of surprise that Jack gave and shot him a warning glance. He knew what his cousin was thinking, but if Zoe wanted to keep working and it made her happy, he would do nothing to stop her. The two sisters had no idea how wealthy both men were. Jack's career as an actor had given him a very good income, all of which he had invested wisely under Daniel's direction. He was also a shareholder in his cousin's lucrative computer company, which is why he had fallen even deeper in love with Libby when she had offered to support him if there were hard times ahead. Daniel himself could have retired at a relatively young age had he chosen to do so, but he enjoyed the challenge of his job, and up until recently work had occupied most of his waking hours. Zoe had changed all that, and now work was an intrusive obstacle, when all he wanted to do was spend his time with her.

Libby and Jack got married in a small Church near to Zoe's parents' house. Although they had tried to keep it low key, the media soon got wind of the wedding and descended in full force, making it a far more hectic affair than any of them would have wished. Jack took it all in his stride, holding Libby protectively to his side, letting the photographers and journalists wander freely about.

"I've found that it's better to smile and let them get on with it," he whispered to Libby. "The sooner they get their pictures, the sooner they'll be gone. Bear up and show them your beautiful teeth."

He was right, the media departed as quickly as they had arrived. Jack had given the reporters a few words to pacify them, allowed the photographers to take as many pictures as they liked and now, they were off, no doubt to print an exaggerated version of events.

Zoe was introduced to Daniel's mother and father and met his two uncles, the fathers of Sylvia and Jack. Although she had met Jack's father before, she had never met Sylvia's father, or Daniel's, and it was fascinating to see these three older men together. She looked from one tall man to another. In spite of their age, they were all still powerfully built and so alike, it was no wonder that their offspring resembled each other so strongly.

Libby looked beautiful, her eyes were luminous, shining with love and happiness as she gazed up at her new husband. Jack looked dazed and his white grin was much in evidence as he gazed back with equal pride at his wife. Zoe felt her heart swell with emotion as she watched the two of them and she frantically fumbled for a tissue, only to find one pressed into her hand.

"I can spare you one of mine, honey," a woman sniffed. It was Daniel's mother, Nancy. "The others are all booked, I'm afraid."

"Thank you." Zoe laughed tremulously. She blotted her eyes carefully, trying not to smudge her mascara. She hoped that she wasn't making too bad an impression on this woman. "They look so happy, don't they?"

"Are you worried about your sister?" His mother studied her flushed face with interest.

"Not really," Zoe replied. "I must admit that I was, but only in the beginning when they first met. Jack's love is so obvious, isn't it?"

Daniel's mother followed her gaze as Zoe looked fondly at her sister. "Yes, I've never seen Jack so at ease, so contented. He has certainly found what he wanted in life, and so it seems has my Daniel." She smiled back at Zoe. "I've been longing to meet you and also very curious."

"Oh, why curious?" Zoe asked warily.

"To see the woman who has captured my son at last." His mother smiled, her face softening at Zoe's anxious expression. She laughed. "Don't worry, I'm not one of these possessive mothers who can't bear to part with her son. In fact, I thought that we would be stuck with him forever. No woman seemed to be good enough as far as he was concerned."

Zoe laughed with her as they stood together watching Daniel approach, a look of suspicion on his face. He stopped in front of them, looking at the two women he loved most in the world, who were both regarding him with varying degrees of love and humour.

"My sixth sense tells me that you were discussing my worst points," he said, his lips twitching.

"How clever of you to have guessed," Zoe giggled.

Daniel dropped a quick kiss on her lips, mindful not to dwell too long on that soft moistness, aware of his mother's watchful eyes. More than once during the evening, Nancy Hammell heard her son's laughter ring out and smiled with satisfaction, happy that her son had found someone who truly loved him. One only had to look at Zoe's face to establish that fact.

The reception was going well, there was much laughter, and the drink flowed freely. Zoe glanced across at her sister, who was talking with their parents. She looked lovely, almost ethereal in her floaty, lace covered dress. Her brown curls cascading down to her shoulders, her face flushed and happy. No one could mistake the look on Jack's face as he constantly glanced about for his wife. Love was something he had never lightly given, and Libby was the one who now held his heart in her hands.

Zoe turned to see where her own true love had gone and found herself looking straight into his eyes. Even from a distance she could see the same expression on Daniel's face as she herself must be showing. That loving look, when each knew they wanted to be alone, and could hardly wait to leave and lose themselves in each other. Those needs would have to keep until the reception was over. Afterwards, time was theirs to spend any way they pleased. Bed appeared to loom large on the horizon.

Zoe noticed that Tom was closely shadowing Sylvia as she made her way from one group of guests to another, introducing him to relatives, with every evidence of being flattered and pleased by his close attention.

Daniel had been separated from Zoe by group of men and now they were gathered around an old piano, which stood to one side of the hall. Jack sat on the stool with Daniel on a chair beside him and began to play. Zoe laughed aloud as one young man, whom she recognised from the small band that had been hired for the event, clamped his hands over his ears with a pained expression. She stood watching the group, a smile still on her face as her sister joined her.

"The boys are having fun, I see," Libby giggled.

"How are you bearing up?" Zoe asked her. "You certainly look happy and radiant."

"I feel wonderful," she cast a loving look at Jack. "I love him so much, Zoe, that I feel as though my heart could burst."

"I know the feeling," Zoe said. "Daniel has a weird and wonderful effect on me. Sometimes I feel as though I'm on a merry-go-round with the emotions he evokes in me."

Suddenly Daniel began to sing in a rich deep baritone, his voice causing goosebumps to rise up all over her body, making her shiver. Zoe caught her sister's eyes, both of them surprised, almost shocked, by this evidence of such talent. Jack suddenly joined in with him, his voice not as deep, but equally as good. Hal, not to be outdone, also joined them, his voice nowhere near as melodious, but still making a good attempt to keep up with them. The brothers sat laughing together with their cousin as they finished the song on an impossibly low note.

Daniel's gaze sought Zoe out and he flushed as he saw her mesmerised expression. He made his way over to them, closely followed by Jack.

"Sorry, girls," he laughed self-deprecatingly at his musical efforts. "We get carried away sometimes. Family gatherings bring out the worst in us."

"It was beautiful," Zoe gave a faint smile. "With voices that good, you can both sing as much as you like, it won't bother me. In fact, it stirs me in the oddest ways."

"Really?" Daniel sidled nearer, his eyes gleaming. "Are you making promises to me again?"

"I might be," she prevaricated.

They were interrupted by his mother, who wanted to introduce Zoe to some latecomers, and were separated once more. By the end of that day, Zoe felt as though she had come to know Daniel's mother very well. She was an attractive and charming woman, who went out of her way to make Zoe's parents feel comfortable and welcome amongst the overpowering Hammell clan. It was apparent that they were a very wealthy family, a fact that had only recently been made clear to Libby and Zoe.

"What you think of them, dad?" she whispered, her arm through her father's.

"Nice people, no side to them, if you know what I mean," he said simply. "Despite their obvious wealth."

He looked around at the huge room that they were standing in, part of a wing that had been rented for the occasion. Jack had insisted on paying a good deal towards the wedding, justifying it by saying that he had so many people to ask to the reception that it was only fair to contribute.

Now, Zoe's father, seeing the sheer opulence of the place and the spread set out on the long elegantly dressed tables lining the room, knew that he couldn't possibly have afforded such a setting. He felt no resentment. The Hammell family had consulted with him every step of the way, and he had to admire their diplomacy. They had made him feel as though it were he doing them a favour, by letting them pay into the wedding.

Zoe smiled as her father laughed down at her and told her about the way he had been so skilfully manipulated. "You'll have to watch out for that Daniel," he grinned. "If he's anything like his mother, you'll find yourself bulldozed into doing exactly what he wants. My advice to you is stand your ground."

"Are you taking my name in vain?" A deep voice interrupted the conversation. Daniel looked into her father's eyes and gave him a knowing man to man look. "Don't worry about me getting my way all the time, I think you know perfectly well by now that I have no defences against your daughter."

"I know that," her father said smugly. "I was just making sure that she was still keeping you under control." Her father left them with a smile and went in search of his wife.

"Are you still under my control?" Zoe giggled, looking up into his dancing green eyes.

"Only just," Daniel agreed. "Although, any minute now, I might whisk you off to my lair."

"You can't," she sniggered. "Your mother is watching you."

"So she is," he sighed, waving across at his parents. He turned and stared down at Zoe, his eyes gleaming with promise. "It seems that I will have to behave myself for now, but later, now that's a different matter."

ꟷ

Two weeks later, Daniel and Zoe also got married, but this time the wedding was a much quieter affair with just close family attending, Jack and Libby having flown over specially for the occasion. Daniel had been his cousin's best man, now Jack in turn was his, standing beside him, two tall handsome men who turned as one when Zoe approached with her father. Her mother watched proudly, surreptitiously wiping the tears away as her husband led her daughter down the aisle. Zoe looked equally as lovely as Libby had on her special day, and the look on Daniel's face as her daughter approached him, assured her of his love. Daniel seemed nervous and fumbled with the ring. She smiled as she saw Zoe reach out and gently touch his hand, finding it amusing that this large powerful man was reduced to a nervous wreck by the occasion, while her slip of a daughter took charge of the situation.

As it happened, Zoe wasn't as calm as she appeared, but sensing Daniel's momentary discomfort gave her confidence as she sought to convey her love to him. He smiled down into her sparkling eyes, relaxing as he saw the message that they held and squeezed her hand, letting his love flow back to her.

Daniel whisked her off on honeymoon abroad, well away from civilisation, where they spent a hectic and unforgettable three weeks laying on the warm sand, frolicking in the sea, just concentrating solely on each other. Now they were home, trying to get back to normal, not easy when all they desired was to remain in bed together.

Chapter Fourteen

Jack was back from America for a month to complete filming on the latest Tronicman adventure. This was to be his last film before launching out into his own production company.

The four of them had met up for lunch at Libby and Jack's hotel. Afterwards the men put a game on and as it was American football, the girls opted out of watching it. Daniel and Jack were immersed in the game, occasionally shouting encouragement at the set, and Libby giggled at her sister's raised brows when Jack jumped up swearing at the screen.

"Take no notice," she sniggered. "It's a boy thing."

Zoe studied her sister. Libby positively glowed, obviously happy in her role as Jack's wife, and she wondered if she herself possessed that same dewy look. She would miss Libby terribly. There were always visits, of course, but they would obviously be limited.

"Come over and stay whenever you wish." Libby looked back at her with a strained smile. Her voice wobbled as she spoke. "I've missed you like crazy."

"I'll take you up on that offer, I promise." Zoe reached out and took her hand, giving it an affectionate squeeze. "Now tell me all your news and I'll tell you mine."

While Libby made more coffee, Zoe sat and observed the antics of the two men, reduced to boyish enthusiasm by the game. She studied Daniel as he talked with Jack and smiled dreamily. His face fascinated her, the strong angles making him look indomitable, a force to be reckoned with. No wonder he did so well in business; he probably simply bulldozed his way through deals with his sheer overpowering presence.

Her reverie was interrupted as Libby returned with the tray of coffee, and they resumed their exchange of gossip. After they had exhausted all avenues of conversation, Zoe stood up and stretched. "I feel like some exercise."

Her voice faltered as she glanced across at the men and caught the warm hungry look in Daniel's watchful eyes. He got up and walked over. "You must be tired."

"It's only three in the afternoon," Zoe protested.

"Okay, then I'm tired," Daniel said, faking a yawn.

"Won't this interrupt your game?" she asked, trying not to smile.

"What game was that?" he looked puzzled, but his eyes were undressing her.

"Daniel," she laughed, her face pink. "What will our hosts think of you?"

Minutes later, Libby stood with Jack, waving them goodbye as they walked to their car.

"I know your cousin likes to read about all the great battles," she smiled, in an aside to Jack, "but I do believe he has met his own Waterloo, don't you?"

Daniel's lips twitched as he overheard the whispered words, and looked down at Zoe's smirk, knowing she had heard them too.

"Come on, Napoleon," she said softly, grabbing his tie and brushing her tongue gently over his top lip, hearing an intake of breath at her provocative action.

"Wait until I get you home," he threatened.

"If I must," she laughed.

She sat quietly beside Daniel on the journey home, knowing he was feeling the same sense of restless anticipation as she was. She loved him so much and knew that her emotions were returned in equal measure by the silent man gripping the steering wheel so tightly, desperate to get home and have her to himself. They never seemed to tire of each other. Oh, she knew that this hectic pace couldn't last, but she wouldn't look too far into the future. She just hoped that their relationship would mature into the same enduring kind of love that her parents shared. She couldn't visualise her life without him.

Daniel left for work the next morning, meaning to organise his day, as opposed to crashing through it as in previous ones in his haste to get home and see Zoe. He got as far as his car and stopped, feeling the pull of her warm body still slumbering in that big soft inviting bed. Zoe was vaguely aware of footsteps pounding up the stairs and turned sleepily to the door. Her eyes opened fully as she saw Daniel standing gazing at her with a purposeful look on his face, and she had a sneaky feeling that she knew exactly what his purpose was. She gave a screech of surprise as he launched himself onto the bed, pinning her down with his patently aroused body.

"Daniel, will you get off me," Zoe moaned, giggling as she tried to wriggle out from beneath him.

"That's the wrong way to reason with me." He gave a weak groan as his body responded to her movements. "Did I hear you say that you had missed me?"

"You haven't given me the chance to say anything yet," she breathed, "and you have only been gone five minutes. Now will you get off me." Zoe wrestled ineffectively in his arms, then lay still.

"Are you giving in that easily?" Daniel loosened his hold and looked down at her, then groaned as he felt her hands unfastening his belt. "Now who's doing the conquering?"

"Just trying to confuse my opponent," she murmured, touching her lips to his throat.

"You are a formidable enemy, Mrs Hammell," he said, with a considering frown. "I will have to think of a better method with which to subdue you."

"This method is quite good," Zoe encouraged him, her voice trembling as she felt his hands push her night dress away and his naked skin pressed against hers. "In fact, it feels quite lethal."

"Right, troops, forward," Daniel said huskily, his voice dying away as he invaded her, killing her brain cells slowly and methodically.

It was some while before sanity crept back and Zoe opened her eyes, giving a faint exhausted laugh. "Get off me, you rampant beast." She pushed at him. "Your army has retreated and before it advances again, what are you doing back here?"

"You don't know?" he asked in mock surprise, laughing as she smacked him on the butt. "I delegated, and my troops can rally whenever you feel like it," he grinned lazily, running his hand lingeringly down her body.

"Boaster," she chuckled at him, stroking his arms. "Your troops deserve a rest, and I must shower and get to work."

"We could share," he offered. "I need a shower."

"Oh, no, you don't," she gurgled as she pulled away and scrambled out of bed. "I know all about you and showers."

She smiled as she locked the bathroom door behind her, remembering the prolonged wash and soap session from the night before. It had taken them an hour and she had been so exhausted when they had finally tumbled into bed that she hadn't even woken when Daniel left for work.

When she emerged, Zoe found him sitting on the end of the bed, looking immaculate once more.

"Mm, you look smart," she purred, running her hands over the broad shoulders, so snugly encased in his suit.

"I can be dishevelled as soon as you like," he offered.

Zoe stood back, her hands resting on his neck and gave him a questioning look. "Why didn't you wake me before you left?"

"My gentlemanly character came to the rescue," he grinned. "I decided that as much as I would like to launch an assault on you, it was only fair to let you sleep in preparation for the next bout."

"Your nobler instincts didn't last long, did they?" she smirked.

"Only as far as the car." He laughed at her flushed face. "Then they evaporated with the daylight and my primal beast let out a roar."

"Control him and go to work," Zoe ordered him as he clamped her between his thighs. "Let me go."

"Oh, very well," he conceded. He leered at her threateningly. "Just remember, I know where to find you now."

"Good," she smiled. "That solves a lot of problems. Although just so as you know, I don't actually live full time in this bed."

He widened his eyes in disbelief. "You don't? Yet, strangely this is always where I find you."

"That might be because you usually manage to whisk me upstairs before I can even say hello," she tittered.

"What better way to tell you how my day has been," he said smugly.

"It might be if we actually got around to talking," Zoe pointed out, laughing as she turned him around and pushed his reluctant body out of the bedroom, tussling with him all the way down the stairs and giggling as she had to prise his fingers off the bannisters. "Go," she commanded, opening the front door.

"Did I tell you about my heat seeking missile?" Daniel asked her hopefully.

"Out," she giggled, swatting at his wandering hands.

Zoe had yet to inform him that he had already put his foot on the ladder to establishing the family name. The next generation was sleeping safely within her, and she wondered how he would react. She knew that he wanted children, but would he want them this soon?

She needn't have worried. When she told him her news later that evening, he held her as though she had presented him with the most precious gift she could bestow. He didn't speak for a long time, and when he did his voice was strangely husky.

"Thank you." He smiled at her, cupping her face between his strong hands. "Now you're doubly precious. I've conquered my reluctant soul mate at last."

"Only because I weakened and sided with you," Zoe protested. "My body is treacherous where you are concerned."

"Good," Daniel grinned, kissing her vigorously. "In that case, I'll keep pressing home my advantage."

"You see," she groaned. "There I go again, letting you do what you like with me."

Zoe felt the rumble of laughter that rippled through the strong body pressed against hers and smiled contentedly, secure in their love as she gave herself up to him, safe in his arms. She could only wonder why she had ever fought him at all.

About the Author

Essa Sims lives in England near the sea. A lifelong lover of painting and reading, she turned to writing as her family gained independence, allowing her to fully embrace her passions.

Romance captivates her the most, and her stories feature rugged heroes and strong-willed heroines whose fiery clashes create exciting, racy interactions. With humour skilfully woven into their lively banter, Essa writes delightful tales that keep readers eagerly turning the pages.

www.ingramcontent.com/pod-product-compliance
Ingram Content Group UK Ltd.
Pitfield, Milton Keynes, MK11 3LW, UK
UKHW041815110325
456069UK00001B/50

* 9 7 9 8 2 3 0 5 6 7 7 1 4 *